Fascinating Wh...
FASCINATING AIDA

Mostly by Dillie Keane

with large contributions from
Adèle Anderson and Nica Burns

ELM TREE BOOKS · LONDON

First published in Great Britain 1986
by Elm Tree Books/Hamish Hamilton Ltd
27 Wrights Lane, London W8 5TZ

Copyright © 1986 by Dillie Keane

Book design by Don Macpherson

British Library Cataloguing in Publication Data

Fascinating Aida (*Group*)
  Fascinating who?
  1. Fascinating Aida (*Group*)
  I. Title
  784.5'0092'2   ML421.F3/

  ISBN 0-241-11925-1

Typeset by Pioneer, Perthshire
Printed and bound in Great Britain
by Billing & Sons Ltd, Worcester

CONTENTS

ACKNOWLEDGMENTS

Special thank you to Marilyn Cutts for three years hard slog and sublime singing.

Second special thank you to Denise Wharmby for coming 12,000 miles. Good luck.

Other debts of gratitude to:

Sam Hutt	for inspiration, help, and knowing when to run out of patience
Michael Clare	for support and sequins
Michael Haeburn-Little	for everything
The Home Office	for the work permit

Also to all the Donmar Warehouse employees, past and present, especially Candace Imison and Toby Moorcroft; to all at Noel Gay; to Julianne White, Michelle Braidman and Alan Turner, Stephen Hetherington and Joseph Seeling, Maria Kempinska, John Moulton, Bruce Talbot, Ian Hughes, Michael Mayhew, Mark Chapman, Nicholas Battle, Lou Wakefield, Angela Pink, Ian Albery, Harry Nash and Lesley Hill.

Thanks to the following for permission to use copyright photographs:

Brian Aris   title page, p.99, 149
Bee Gilbert   p.14
Michael Mayhew   p.18, 44, 58-9, 67, 84, 88, 91, 103, 120, 129, 132, 140-1, 155, 156, 159, 160
London Weekend Television   p.55, 142
David Liddle   p.138
Michael Cumpper   p.50, 71, 133
Ged Murray   p.72
Michael Norris   p.74 main picture
Tim O'Sullivan   p.118

and to all the newspapers who gave us permission to quote articles and reviews. Every effort has been made to trace copyright holders we apologise for any omissions and will be pleased to make due acknowledgment in any subsequent editions.

The lyrics of 'My Favourite Tool' by Dillie Keane and Marilyn Cutts are reproduced by permission of EMI Music Publishing Ltd and International Music Publications.

Finally thanks to Mr Brocklebank of The Crown, Seven Dials, London WC2; and Michael Belben of Smiths Restaurant, Covent Garden, London WC2 for letting us take photographs on the premises, and to Nicholas Justin for being our waiter.

CHAPTER ONE

IN WHICH THREE OF US MEET AT A JUNCTION

If you're Irish, it is highly likely that Crewe Station will become a significant landmark in your life. It is about half way between Euston and Holyhead, and there seems to be a genetic necessity in the Irish character to spend a great deal of time and money catching the night train and mailboat to London or Dublin – probably the result of 800 years of programming. As a Genuine, Portsmouth-born, Pedigree Mick, Crewe Station had figured large in my life as a depressing landmark where I always woke up with a hangover. British Rail had often turfed me out there to change trains for no apparent reason in the dead of a wintry night, and junctions don't come much dingier than Crewe between 3.00 and 6.00 am. It's the Beachy Head of the North – a cracker of a place to top yourself.

Had you therefore suggested to me that I'd spend over half a year living in a pestilential hovel on the bridge over the railway at Crewe in pursuit of my art, I'd have recommended a good nursing home. And yet here I was in August 1979 returning for another term of punishment – a second season at Crewe Rep.

My friend Tom Mannion, who was in the company, once described Crewe as being like a seaside town in winter without any sea. That's a little on the flattering side, but you get the picture. Apart from the two big industries (British Rail and Rolls Royce), there's a big market there which is terrific if you've run out of lime green cuddly toys, rainbow drops by the kilo or fluorescent fur-trimmed parkas. At least it's colourful, which is more than can be said for the rest of the town. There's a fairly miserable parade of shops, one or two greasy caffs, a couple of hopeless cinemas, a few dingy pubs, and as much bingo as a body could want. And of course, there's the celebrated Crewe Alexandra, which for years has occupied a unique place at the bottom of the fourth division.

Finally, Crewe has a lovely, if crumbling, Victorian theatre complete with red plush, flock wallpaper and gilt cupids. I was told there had once been six such theatres in the town, but they were pulled down one by one as Variety gradually died, the industries fell away making spare cash even scarcer and taking the heart out of the town, and television took over as the opium of the people. The Lyceum should have been demolished too on the evidence of the attendance figures – 30% capacity was a really cracking night out of the pantomime season – but people are sentimental about their theatres and a small yet solid band of burghers fought to keep it open, so it limped painfully on on a couple of inadequate grants from the Arts Council and the impoverished local council. If it had only been sited at Nantwich, a town just a few miles down the road which is awash with bijou gift shops and up-market card boutiques, it might have stood a chance. As it was, it would have been better to have ditched the repertory company altogether and turned the venue over to wrestling promoters, because you couldn't even guarantee an audience for the O Level set Shakespeare.

Still, in 1979 I was full of naïve hope that a sizzling season of brilliant productions would have the *Crewe Chronicle* in ecstasies and the townsfolk beating down the door for tickets.

We were to open with *The Boyfriend* by Sandy Wilson, followed by *Charley's Aunt* (Brandon Thomas), *A Mad World, My Master's* (Barrie Keeffe), *Romeo and Juliet, The Ghost Train* (written by the wonderful Arnold Ridley of *Dad's Army* fame: he sold the rights to the play outright in the twenties for about a fiver and never made a penny more from the huge number of productions and films.) Finally, there was the Christmas Panto, *Puss in Boots*.

I was to be one of the few employed for the full season, and I had a heady string of geriatric roles to play starting with Madame Dubonnet and finishing with the Witch. In those days, I was prematurely quite grey, a characteristic inherited from my mother, and had a tendency to do other actresses twice my age out of a job. However, it was at Crewe that I first started to dye my hair in earnest and start the long journey to becoming a natural blonde.

True to form, I arrived late for the first read-through. I had been spending my last few days of freedom in Dublin and dear old British Rail had decided that I was better off sitting at Holywell Junction for several hours than proceeding on to Crewe. Consequently I arrived flustered, my mascara half way down my cheeks (I always blub when I'm frustrated), my special make-a-good-impression clothes crushed, and my hat awry. (I'm a strong believer in wearing hats to first read-throughs: it stops my hair standing on end in sheer terror.) I leapt out of my taxi and blew into the theatre like a rotary storm. Too late: the read-through was over, and the cast were all having a getting-to-know-you drink in the bar before sloping off to have a getting-off-with-each-other drink in the pub. I made the sort of grand entrance you'd expect from a demented chicken, and everybody instantly assumed that I was quite off my chump.

I was in such a tizz that the only person I can remember talking to that day was a small, dark, serious girl with an extremely dry sense of humour. She turned out to be Marilyn Cutts who was playing Polly Browne ('with an "e"!'), the juvenile lead in *The Boyfriend*.

We had an odd, stilted conversation in which we exchanged the dull facts of our recent past.

I broke off in the middle of a sentence and looked blankly at her.

'You don't want to know all this,' I said. 'This is all incredibly boring.'

'Yes, of course it is,' she replied, 'but we've got to get it all out of the way first and then we can get down to the real business of making friends.' Eminently sensible, I thought, impressed. I was even more impressed when I heard her sing.

Gradually I got to know the rest of the company, some of whom I already knew from the previous season. First there was the stunningly good-looking Artistic Director, David Sumner, who could have given Omar Sharif a run for his winnings. He was a rather brilliant, unhappy man with a remarkable gift for picking good actors but was suffering from the effects of living in Crewe for three years in a row. By the time we joined the company, the consistently empty houses and the rock solid apathy of the townsfolk had ground away most of his hopes and dreams, and he was at times very hard to reach.

Once, I went to watch the local amateur group who for a couple of weeks a year got the theatre for a peppercorn rent. Their production this time was *Oliver*, and there wasn't a single seat to be had in the house. It was jammed to the rafters with mums, aunties, friends of the seamstresses and cousins of the set-builders. I stood watching at the back, my disbelief growing every second.

For a start it was obvious that every boy from the age of four to fourteen within a twenty five mile radius of the town was in it (and some with obvious reluctance) because they were so squashed that they were almost falling like lemmings into the orchestra pit. As Fagin was played by an unusually small man who stooped a great deal in his interpretation of the role, he was therefore indistinguishable from his youthful band of larcenists for the major part of the evening, especially as the follow-spot operator seemed to favour the roaming searchlight style of illumination rather than focus on any one character for any length of time. (Perhaps he'd learned his lighting style from watching old war films.) Then when you could see Fagin it was clear that while he was reviewing the situation, so was his beard. He spent much of the night holding it on with his hand which, coupled with his tendency to sing at the floor on account of his hunch, didn't do much for his projection. Scenery fell down, a backdrop got stuck halfway between the floor and the flies and remained there as hundreds of hapless lads shuffled trancelike on and off. Entrances were missed, words forgotten, boys got left behind on stage and stood dolefully picking their noses as they waited to be rescued by their chums – 'Gavin, *come on! Gavin! We're not supposed to be on now!*' Nancy came on to save the evening with *As Long As He Needs Me*, tripped on her shawl and fell flat on her face. It was a truly diabolical show.

As I left the theatre somewhere near midnight, I overheard two middle-aged ladies talking about the show.

'Oh,' said one, 'wasn't it lovely?'

'Yes,' said the other, 'and so much better than the professionals.'

It's no wonder David was unhappy.

Our choreographer was also in the show playing Madcap Maisie. She was a small, black-haired, curvy girl with more energy than I'd ever seen in anyone. Her name was Nica Burns and she was like an extremely busy bird, all bustling feathers and sharp eyes. She was a pretty good choreographer, especially since it was her first big musical, and the more one found out about her, the more fascinating she became. For a start she turned out to be half Scots and half Hispanic-Greco-Jewish which explained the Latin looks and the unfair helping of Continental sex-appeal which has grown men weeping and policemen turning in their badges. She had a law degree from London University, had taught dance, had been to drama school, had become an actress who quickly graduated to choreographer. Not bad for twenty four years old. Depressingly dynamic, in fact.

I was quite wary of Nica to start with. The first thing she did was to make an announcement.

'Listen, everybody!' she shouted, and blew the whistle that hung permanently around her neck and which she used mercilessly during rehearsals whenever you put your feet in the wrong place. 'I want to call the whole cast tonight at 9.30.'

The whole cast to be called at 9.30 *at night*? A murmur ran round the room.

'I want to see you all at Ray's Place, and Keith is the only one who's excused because he has a family to go to.'

'What's Ray's Place, Nica?' said someone nervously.

'It's the local disco. I want to be able to see how you all dance. And nobody's allowed to sit out. Okay?'

We all thought she was quite barmy, but we trooped dutifully along to the disco that night – well, nobody was brave enough to refuse – and danced energetically while she sat and made notes. 'Sorry, Gina, I haven't seen enough of you!' she cried, as an exhausted girl limped off the floor. 'Dillie, stop dancing with Tom! I need to see him with Marilyn.'

'She's on the floor with Mike, Nica.'

'Well, she's not supposed to be. Tell her to come here immediately and . . . what on earth is Janthea doing with her arms? Loveday, you've had quite enough cocktails: get back on that floor! Well, bring your handbag with you . . . You can dance with Jo, she's free. . . . I'm warning you, Loveday . . .'

At last she was satisfied and went away home, and Ray's Place began to live up to its advertisements as 'The Place Where Romance Begins'.

I was so nervous of Nica that I worked like a demon to impress her and ended up playing Madame Dubonnet at an angle of about 60 degrees – a human Leaning Tower of Pisa. But she obviously thought (like my mother) that at twenty seven I was well over the hill because one day she looked at me in the dressing room as I stood there in my knickers and said in a voice full of innocent wonder 'Gosh Dillie! You've got an *awfully* good body for twenty seven.' I think she expected my bosom to be flapping around my ankles.

Then there was an extraordinary plump boy called Fitz who had jet black hair, wonderful Vivien Leigh eyes with outrageously long lashes, and more freckles than he had skin for. He was in the chorus for the first show as *The Boyfriend* doesn't have a lot of parts for roly-poly chaps with sloe eyes ('I'm the fat one in pink!' he'd cry), but was going on to play a string of roles in the other plays.

16 (Cp. 2) — THE CHRONICLE, THURSDAY, SEPT. 6, 1979.

Boyfriend woos the audiences

by Colin Roberts

"THE BOY FRIEND", now on at Crewe's Lyceum Theatre, is a first-rate entertainment.

It is a captivating composition of bright song and dance with an intertwined love story.

The enthusiasm and skilful management of the varied routines by the young cast adds to the general lustre.

There is nothing profound about it. You just sit back and enjoy nicely sung songs, good acting, and the exuberance of it all.

It is about a young girl at a finishing school — she is the daughter of a millionaire — who falls for a penniless messenger boy.

There are poignant moments between the young lovers, upsets because of parental objections and swelling happiness when the boy's real identity becomes known.

Some quite excellent performances are given.

The vivacious Marilyn Cutts is a superb Polly Browne. She puts such energy and expression into the part and a bonus is that she does sing well.

Tom Mannion injects real feeling into his role of the boyfriend and as Hortense, the French maid, the attractive Loveday Oakley is ooh la la!

Bouquets must go to Nica Burns, the show's choreographer, and Dillie Keane.

Nica, playing Maisie, a sweet young thing, puts tremendous vigour into the dancing part of her role and Dillie stamps real character into the part of Madame Dubonnet.

Jack Carr is good as the randy Lord Brockhurst and Janthea Williams, Gina Rowe and Joanne Zorim please as the pretty, giggling school girls.

It is a show full of sparkle and a pleasure to watch.

Fitz is larger than life, even now he's slim, and the first time I talked to him I thought he was quite dotty. He came over to the table where I was sitting, plonked himself down and said in an utterly mesmerising and beautifully modulated voice: 'Hello, I'm Michael Fitzgerald, but please call me Fitz, everyone does. *Do* tell me *all* the gossip – I'm sure you know *everything*! I know we're going to be great friends!'

He was quite right.

I found digs with a Mrs Moore.

'I would have preferred a policeman,' she told me; 'I find them very nice.' But since homeless bluebottles were thin on the ground that season she would make do with me. I didn't last long with Mrs Moore – I was thrown out on my ear when she discovered I had mangled her slipper in the wringer after flooding the kitchen.

'It's the last straw,' she said, shaking with anger. 'You come in here at all hours; you bring goodness knows what kind of people into the house, actors and all sorts, and then you destroy my slipper! I knew I should have waited for a policeman.'

I moved into what was known as 'Theatre House' because the council, who owned it, had given it over to the theatre for the use of the actors. This was by no means a generous move on the council's part because to describe it simply as Dickensian would be a serious underestimation. Not even Zola could encompass such squalidness. It wasn't just a shithole, it was the Versailles of shitholes, the Taj Mahal of hovels. It was Dante's vision of hell, St John's abomination

Above, left: Dillie (not yet a natural blonde) and Nica (the only time she's ever knelt to Dillie) in Charley's Aunt.

Above, right: Where are the sequins? Where is the tinsel? Dillie as Grandma Sprightly in A Mad World, My Master's.

of desolation, and the slums of Rio all rolled into one. Wallpaper peeled obscenely from the walls, dirt crawled noisomely round the skirtings, putrid green slime oozed from underneath the fridge, cockroaches nested in the cupboards and mice ran riot everywhere. Rats frolicked round the unspeakable ordure rotting rankly in the garden but it didn't matter – you couldn't see through the windows for grime.

There were five of us in the house: Tom Mannion, straight from Drama School in Glasgow, fresh-faced and very overawed. He's currently playing excellent roles at the RSC and in his turn probably overawing fresh-faced youths straight from drama school. Then there was Mike Fenner, a glorious piece of beefcake much swooned over by various girls about town, and last heard of hanging upside down, naked and covered with mud in *The Romans in Britain* at the National Theatre; Janthea Williams, a tall, gentle, willowy girl who looked like a *Vogue* twenties cartoon and had survived bouncing down a Peruvian ravine in a car after it had slipped off a mountain road: she won second prize in a *Woman's Own* Short Story Competition during her time with us and lived with her mother in North Wales in a house with a real ghost that threw a picture at Mike Fenner's knee when we were all at lunch there – it was most alarming, especially when it stamped about upstairs for no apparent reason; and Hermann, a Dutch ballet dancer.

Nica and Marilyn were in digs together down the road with a Mrs Barron who was altogether more congenial than Mrs Moore and didn't mind them not being rozzers. Tom used to call them 'The Accident Unit' as together their surnames were Cutts and Burns. Marilyn was at that time a recent convert to Weight Watchers and was eagerly trying to evangelise Nica. This didn't go down too well with Nica as she didn't think she needed to go on a diet. Undaunted, Marilyn made her a Weight Watchers cake which was so tiny that Nica ate half at one sitting, thinking that this was her portion. She never heard the end of it – Marilyn was most put out as it was supposed to do the two of them for ten days, and she had to borrow next week's butter allowance for several months before she caught up again.

On the second day, rehearsals began in earnest. So did the problems. Nica was away for the first week so Hermann, who was her assistant, took charge. Unfortunately he was classically trained and couldn't tell a Charleston from a Turkey Trot and had us struggling in agony for days with slow pliés and arabesques. Also, while the cast were a talented enough bunch, singing was not overall their strong point.

Chaos set in. Joanne Zorian, an irrepressibly funny girl in the chorus, wrote 'Hi!' on her front teeth with a make-up pencil so every time she smiled at people the rehearsals broke up. Loveday Fraser Oakley's King Charles Spaniel, Amun Hotep, tried to join in all the dance routines. Bernard Collins hated musicals, and stood about looking depressed. Janthea was about a foot taller than the other girls in the chorus and felt depressed. We all went for our costume fittings, and then everybody felt depressed.

Then Nica arrived, took charge, and managed to galvanise us into some sort of shape. However, audiences peaked at around 18% capacity. The costumes and set were against us. The designer had designed a huge octagonal platform like a christening cake for centre stage and we had to leap three feet to get on to it. The choreography suffered a bit because any time anyone tripped it caused a major pile-up. It got cut down to a manageable size in the end but not before Nica had threatened hysterics. Then the wardrobe department had been massively overstretched and the costumes were upholstery rather than couture with the ladies either looking like animated lampshades or all-in wrestlers.

The high point for me was when Marilyn and I sang our first duet together: 'Poor Little Pierrette'. It's a haunting little song – in fact, every single song in that show is a winner – and our voices were very well matched. (That was before my next career as a wine bar chanteuse ruined my voice forever.) As Marilyn said, there wasn't a dry seat in the house.

The season limped on. Productions were put on and the audience stayed away in droves except for *A Mad World, My Master's* as news had leaked through the town that Loveday would be removing her clothes for her art. Then all sorts of people turned up who'd never been to the theatre in their lives.

People came and went with their address books slightly fuller. Marilyn and Nica fled after a couple of months. The TIE group (Theatre in Education) folded after one show attracted an audience of precisely nil and the miserable actors were seen sobbing in the pub. A discontented company stirred up union trouble which went nowhere. The 'Save Crewe Theatre Fund' was started to revive inert morale. Morale stayed inert, even after my own wildly successful Christmas raffle. Winter set in, and the rain, sleet and snow started to seep in through the cracked panes of the windows in Theatre House. You couldn't escape it even backstage because the theatre was in nearly as bad a state as our house. Not even the prospect of the January sale at Etam's could cheer me.

By Christmas there were very few of the original bunch left and during panto I spent most of the time getting tight on Martinis with the Mums of the local dance troupe while their Wee Twinkling Wonders did their acrobatic icicle and tapping rabbit routines to the delight of the audiences. I got on extremely well with the Mums and they undoubtedly kept me sane during the apparently endless panto – I used to sit under the stage with them all through the show, face covered in green goo, sipping cocktails and discussing the merits of front loaders as opposed to twin tubs, and I still hear from quite a few of the kids themselves who of course are all teenagers now . . .

I hate panto. I was a very disgruntled witch especially as I had wanted to play Principal Boy and be loved, but Pattie Coldwell steamed in and stole the part from under my thigh boots. I did forgive her when I found out she had wanted to play the witch, but I shall never forget the faint smell of weewee wafting from endless rows of terrified kiddiewinkles wetting themselves every time I came on. Nothing on earth would induce me to do it ever again, not even if Harrison Ford was playing the Prince. All that ghastly bonhomie, the exhausted mothers, the bankrupted fathers, the over-excited, over-Christmassed brats, the monstrous Brownie packs, each dib-dib-dibber armed with a family sized bag of crisps . . . There are actors who say they love panto, but there can surely only be one reason for it – all those extra performances spell O-V-E-R-T-I-M-E. And typically, Crewe lived up to its reputation as we had to cancel almost all of the extra performances due to – what else? – lack of interest.

Don't get me wrong – I wouldn't have missed that season at Crewe for all the world. I met Marilyn and Nica for one thing, and learned an awful lot about acting. And all that depression must have been terribly character forming.

And there's one other thing that I learned at Crewe that I shall never forget. There was an actor there called Peter Cleall who used to say that the stages in a successful actor's life could be summed up in five questions.

1) Who's John Smith?
2) You know who might be good for this part? John Smith!
3) You know who we've got to have for this part? John Smith!
4) You know who would have been good for this part? John Smith.
5) Who's John Smith?

It's true.

Panto over, I left Colditz on the down train and went to find solace in the company of the only people who understood – the former inmates.

CHAPTER TWO

AFTER COLDITZ

I knew Marilyn for three and a half years and Lizzie, the other original member, for eight, before we started Fascinating Aïda.

For both of them any projects we undertook were strictly to fill the periods of unemployment. Even when we got the group started, it was only a hobby to them. And though I was certain that if I could only persuade the two of them, that we had something special when we worked together, I didn't quite know for a long time what the hell it was that we should actually do, apart from stand up and sing songs which didn't seem at all original. It was faith without a vision, and so we pussyfooted around one another for ages before FA came into being.

Back down in London, I slowly readapted to civilian life, meeting up with old friends, and after several months I noticed that nearly all the people I saw regularly were my fellow ex-Crewets: it wasn't just me – there were twelve of us who kept in contact on a daily basis. It was then I developed my Colditz theory which was simply that the experience had been so numbingly ghastly that when it was all over, we couldn't live without seeing one another and had to go on meeting in the Green Man in Piccadilly like ex-POWs.

One old friend who stayed the course of my rehabilitation was Lizzie Richardson, a Canadian girl who was my best pal from drama school days. We had once shared a flat, and she and I used to sing duets together for fun and occasional remuneration.

This had started in a curious way. Lizzie and I had sung together a little when we were at drama school: we shared the same singing teacher who encouraged us to sing classical duets. I thought Lizzie had a lovely voice and when we harmonised her sweetness and strength covered up my deficiencies. (Yet I could never sing duets with Marilyn other than that first one in Crewe – as her voice got better and better and mine got steadily worse, singing together only made her sound divine and me sound like a frog being crushed under the door.) Lizzie left drama school a year ahead of me, and I only saw her from time to time. Then in my last summer holiday before my final year, I landed a job in Sweden for two months playing piano and singing in a late night bar in Stockholm.

One night in Sweden I had a terrible dream about Lizzie: she was lonely, destitute, and living in a women's hostel. I went to visit her and found her lying reading on a bunk in a large dormitory. I tried to talk to her but she just turned to me and said bitterly 'Don't come near me: you didn't help me when I really needed you: it's too late now.' Then she turned to her book again and refused to look at me.

Well, the dream was so frighteningly vivid that although I don't normally set great store by my paranormal powers – I have all the psychic ability of a spirit kettle – I wrote to her that day in great alarm, telling her of my dream and asking if she was all right. She answered by return and said yes, she was at an all time low and wondering whether she should abandon her hopes of working in England and go back to Canada as she was having no luck getting a job that would give her an Equity card. Lizzie also said in her letter that she'd have written before if she'd had my address as she knew I was getting my card with this Swedish job through the Variety end of Equity: could I possibly help her?

Getting an Equity card is the ultimate in Catch 22 – in order to get a job, you have to have a union card, and in order to get a union card you have to have a job. There is a quota of new actor members allowed in each year but it is far smaller than the number of people trying to get in. Which only goes to show how absurd the criteria are for getting an Equity card – when I applied for mine I produced a grubby little piece of paper which said that I had been playing the piano and singing for two months in a bar in Stockholm, and this constituted a valid contract that got me into the union with no bother at all, because if you can juggle, eat fire, get sawn in half and show them a contract that proves you've been working for a certain length of time, you get in. But Lizzie and countless others who've been through three gruelling years of drama school come out at the end of their courses with not even a toehold in the business.

Back to the story. On my return to England, Lizzie and I met up and rehearsed a few standard numbers (endless Porter and Gershwin) with me singing the harmonies and we managed to get ourselves a handful of gigs at one of the Flanagan's establishments in Surrey. We took a train to Oxted where we were fetched by the manageress. Then we'd arrive at the restaurant, and wait to start singing. It was an extraordinary gig because nobody ever went there – the pub at the other end of the building had men in three piece suits hanging from the rafters but the restaurant was a morgue. We were there to attract customers who put their noses round the door, but since nobody did that either we sat alone and bemused in a cavernous dining hall.

The job didn't last too long and it didn't advance Lizzie's career one whisker but it cheered her up and shortly afterwards she got a job at the Bristol Old Vic which cheered her up even more. We continued to warble at parties and so when I escaped from the Crewe Lyceum we teamed up again.

After Crewe, I had to find gainful employment and quick as the duns were massing on the stairs. Marilyn and Nica had sailed into other acting jobs but my face didn't fit anyone's bill. So by day I typed up articles on brachiating chimpanzees and aposematic coloration in moths for a wildlife photographer in West Hampstead, and by night I returned to my sometime occupation of wine bar pianist. I had a variety of regular gigs, most of them ghastly, the least bearable being a chi-chi little joint down Mayfair way much frequented by disc-jockeys, the minor nobility and rich Arabs. It was the kind of place where a good looking girl with a head for business could save for her old age, and even I had quite a number of opportunities while I was there to rise below my station.

At the other end of the scale was Shades, my local wine-bar where I was to delight my neighbours every Friday night with my renditions of 'Stardust' and 'Kitchen Man'. Shades, named after the proprietress's Dad's sunglasses which adorned his handsome nose day and night, rain or shine, was fifty yards from my front door, a handy distance for an inebriate chanteuse. It was owned by an eccentric couple called Des and Jackie, she small, pregnant and Jewish, he tall, charming and West Indian. Between them they attracted the widest mixture of types I've ever seen in any regular clientele – black, white, poor, rich, gay, straight, Sloanie, brickie – they all came and no-one felt out of place or got bothered. If there was any trouble, just one word from Jackie and it was over. It was as if Shades was the community centre: you could always be sure of a friendly ear if you went down there on your own needing a bit of company. Which is what made it doubly distressing when they started getting aggro from the National Front who, as self-appointed guardians of our xenophobia, decided that the racial mix of a Jewish girl and a black guy was too offensive to stand a minute longer in the pleasant hinterland of British West Hampstead. So they broke down the door, smashed the plate glass window a couple of times and started to make life unbearable. Des and Jackie kept going, but when one of the guys who worked there – black as well – got stabbed to death on the way home one night by a white thug, they started to lose heart in the enterprise.

When I started playing there, it had just opened and was just building up its clientele. I was going quietly dippy with the tedium of providing live muzak to drunken tone-deaf groovers five nights a week, so I suggested that I bring in some musical friends to liven things up. Des and Jackie were enthusiastic, so Lizzie and I brushed up our duets and a girl called Carola Stewart came to do some three-part harmony with us. Carola is Sloane Square's answer to Bette Midler. A big, enthusiastic and noisy blonde bombshell exploding with pzazz, she had more energy than our two foot square of stage allowed and I developed a natty way of bashing her with my right hand on the fourth beat of every bar whenever she stood in front of me while still keeping time with my left hand. She was a good singer and what's more, a good harmonist (the two don't necessarily go hand in hand) and good naturedly put up with my quirky choice of songs.

There were six regulars in all: as well as Lizzie, Carola and myself we featured Lindsay, our lady trumpeteuse, and Marilyn who set ears a-sizzlin' with 'A-Tisket, A-Tasket' and other standards. She was featuring in *The Doctor's Dilemma* at Greenwich at the time, and by the interval she'd gone to join the butler in that Great Pantry in the Sky or wherever, and Act Two found her knitting in her lonely dressing-room awaiting that brief moment of glory at the curtain call when the citizens of Greenwich would roar as one: 'We want the moron in the mob cap!' (Marilyn claims that 80% of her acting career was spent playing morons in mob caps.) On Fridays, however, she was willing to cheat the citizens and as soon as her body had been discovered trussed up in the drinks cabinet or wherever Shaw usually puts his victims, she'd leap out of her corset and into her car, and drive up to West Hampstead like a bat out of hell.

Finally, there was Eddie the saxophone player, a heavily bearded septuagenarian South African who always wore shorts. He came up to me one night and said in a thick South African accent: 'You not a musician, but you don't play bum notes. Nex' week Ah bring mah sax. Ah play wuth you, jah. Real music.' And he did, and to be honest he was the best musician there. But he was a mysterious cove and not fond of answering questions about himself, so we never found anything out about him, except that his kissing days were far from over.

Mad as it was, the combination worked. Everyone got their turn, and we occasionally produced some really nice music.

We laboured under the name 'Shame'. This was due to a private joke derived from one of my seven South African flatmates who used the word indiscriminately to express amazement of any kind. Thus if you told her something serious like you'd lost your entire family in a plane crash in the Swiss Alps or the electricity bill had arrived, 'Shame!' she'd wail, dripping with sympathy. Conversely, were you to announce that you had become a Littlewoods millionaire overnight, 'Shame!' she'd cry, eyes a-twinkle with delight on your behalf.

Finding the right name for a group is like looking at a field full of haystacks and hoping there's a needle in one of them. 'Shame' as a

name was, I admit, a stinker but then it wasn't ever a serious contender as a permanent handle for the group for the sole reason that nobody took the group seriously. The collective ambition to be a hit with plonk drinkers further afield in Cricklewood and Camden was a little wanting: Shades was empire enough.

It was during this time that I wrote my first song since my prolific schooldays. I had penned my first proper air at the age of twelve, a song extolling the virtues of my incredibly groovy Dollyrocker dress which was a snappy red and blue check thing that was *almost* a mini and guaranteed to make the wearer feel like Cathy McGowan. Frocks have always been a big inspirational source.

Later, I was destined for prominence in the Convent of the Sacred Heart Pop Club and I cut a disc at the tender age of sixteen – I was a guitarist and choir member on the recording of Frances Hunter-Gordon's sublimely trendy Folk Mass, which we made at the very EMI studios in Abbey Road that the Beatles made so famous and someone said that George Martin was doing the mixing. I believed it for years until I looked at the sleeve.

My big moment came when I had three entries in the Inaugural School Pop Concert – the nuns were pretending to be desperately liberal at that time and encouraged heavily supervised jamborees such as this but there's not a lot you can get up to on a Thursday night with 300 girls in 700 acres of Sunny Surrey Hills, so the Pop Concert was a woefully tame affair. Still I was pretty thrilled when my songs came second, third and fifth, though it was a bitter blow to be pipped by Green and Inky singing their self-penned smash hit 'Robots'. Mind you, 'Robots' was a great deal more mainstream than either 'Dream' or 'Swinging Little Muddletown on the Puddlemarsh', my compositions which were a bit fanciful – a lesson I still haven't learned.

I did go on writing songs at school but I was terribly unhappy there and looking back at some of the lyrics I've kept I wonder that I'm still alive at all. They're all about being dead and making people sorry for what they've done to me, in true adolescent style, and show a remarkable talent for self-dramatisation. I also set quite a lot of poetry to music there but I never kept it, which I regret.

After school I went to Dublin to read music at Trinity College and lost confidence completely. My musical talent is 100% thistledown. I have a genius for flummery. Now my faculty were deeply serious: much valuable time was spent studying lugubrious sixteenth century motets for sackbut and flugelhorn when one could have been better occupied finding out what won the 3.30 at Phoenix Park. And these bozos in charge of my future considered Tchaikovsky to be the musical equivalent of Barbara Cartland and

Lizzie Richardson, the sort of girl who looks wonderful first thing in the morning — rats!

even Beethoven was a bit suspect – the Jean Plaidy of the Symphony? The whole Romantic Movement was utterly discounted as a ghastly aberration from which we were only properly rescued by Schoenberg. Now to me, Schoenberg stinks. Schoenberg's a pill. Can you hum Schoenberg? No. Do you come away from a Schoenberg gig thinking God's in his heaven and all's well with the world? No. Is it music to commit suicide by? Yes. It makes Leonard Cohen sound like 'Rustle of Spring'.

The professor despaired of me when I begged him to include Duke Ellington in our studies and used to shake his head mournfully, and say 'You should have gone to York . . .' in a manner that wouldn't have flattered the faculty at York much. I finally fell from grace when I innocently declared that Johann Strauss and Arthur Sullivan were my favourite composers. Forever cheap, me.

I recently met my lecturer, a delightful man called Dr Groocock, in Dublin. I stopped him in the street and when he looked blankly at me, I reminded him of who I was.

'And what are you doing now?' he asked, fully expecting I think to hear that I was working as a music copyist and married with a tribe of tone-deaf kids.

'I'm a musician!' I said, realising that Fascinating Aïda was far too complicated to explain to a man in a hurry. 'I write songs to commission for the BBC.'

'Good Lord!' he gasped. 'You made good!'

I left Trinity early after a long illness had prevented me from taking my exams – it gave me an excuse not to go on with a degree I hated, and I never looked at a piece of manuscript paper until I wrote 'Get Knotted' during our reign at Shades. (I'd burned all the drivel I wrote at University.) It came to me in the middle of the night while staying at my sister's house. I was lying in bed thinking about an old boyfriend and I suddenly realised with a burst of joy that I was no longer a heartbroken wretch. 'I wouldn't have you back upon a silver dish,' I thought. 'I wouldn't have you back if I could make a wish . . . hmmm, that rhymes. . . .' I thought: '. . . so I'm off to fry some other fish??? . . . yes, that'll do . . . so baby (ooh ooh?) Get Knotted??? . . . Yes . . . get knotted, that's ok . . . gosh, I must write that down.'

And Lo! A Song Was Born! It wasn't exactly 'Ev'ry Time We Say Goodbye I Cry a Little' but at least it wasn't 'One Step Ahead of the Posse', and in its original version it was a fiesty little numero that went down a storm at Shades. It was hotly followed by 'Red Hot Baby', another scorcher of my own which would have put paid to 'Robots' if only I'd written it in time.

Lizzie, Carola and I managed to get one proper gig during all that time – we were booked for one of the Sunday night Variety Shows at the Theatre Royal, Stratford East. We were to do four songs in two lots of two and that was our total repertoire at the time. The piano was a tone flat all over, so to compensate I had to transpose up a tone. Our first two songs went down fine on adrenalin alone, but by the time we got on to do our second set we were all a bit tight. I forgot to transpose and we sounded like the Paul Robeson Memorial Glee Club. The audience took the opportunity to greet long lost friends and go to the toilet. It was glaringly obvious that we hadn't got much to offer other than our enthusiasm, and we couldn't agree at all on a style of dress, had no choreography and no presentation at all. We weren't asked back.

I also got some solo alternative cabaret gigs, but I hadn't much idea. Jack Klaff, Lizzie's boyfriend, had written a hilarious poem for me about the frustration of the spear-carrier's lot in the R.S.C. and he'd helped me with a couple of pieces I'd written – they were very funny but suited to being performed in a theatre rather than a pub and I didn't ever feel at home on the alternative cabaret circuit as a solo performer. I used to describe myself as an alternative alternative comedienne because I only ever got booked at 5.30 pm on the day of the gig when everyone else was sick, dead, or gone to Bognor.

After a few months of doing every Friday at Shades, people either got bored or jobs. I eventually got a proper job too and dropped all my piano gigs. But the seed which was later to become FA had been planted and I was quietly determined to get a three-part harmony women's group together at some stage in my life.

LADY IN WAITING

Adèle takes up the story . . .

In 1979, when Dillie, Marilyn and Nica were wowing them in Crewe, I was working as a civil servant. My full title was Executive Officer Training Opportunities Advisor for part of the South London area, a patch stretching from Brixton through Vauxhall to South Norwood.

In those days the government was pouring money into training, hoping to ease the chronic unemployment in that part of London. My career as a servant of Her Majesty up until this point had not been a happy or successful one. I had enjoyed being sent away on residential training courses at the taxpayer's expense, but when it came to doing the job for which I had been trained, nothing I'd learned seemed to work, I'd been unceremoniously moved from two departments already, and I don't suppose the Training Services Agency relished the thought of taking me on, given my track record.

But I found my feet here. I enjoyed the work and it appears I did it well. I spent most of my days away from the office conducting interviews at various colleges and, once the courses were running, dropping in some times to check everything was progressing smoothly. I got to know some of the students quite well, particularly those who took a Preparatory or an ESL (English as a Second Language) course prior to full training.

I cut a colourful figure around the colleges. Often I wore a huge yellow jacket, a purple skirt and fluorescent green ankle socks in which to conduct my interviews. Well, I was dealing with a lot of youngsters and I was determined not to be the conventional civil servant.

I had never wanted to be a civil servant at all. I'd wanted to be an actor, or, more precisely, a famous actor, for as long as I could remember. I recall when I was fifteen (such a great age: everything was illegal but you did it anyway) telling anyone who would listen, 'I'm going to be a star!' But just to hedge my bets, I would add 'and if I don't make it by the time I'm thirty, I'm going to kill myself!' (I'm staying 29 until further notice.) When Olivia Hussey was chosen by Zeffirelli to play Juliet I was sick with jealousy and only a little less irrational when, a few

Adèle recreates her rôle as a Civil Servant. (The effect is more startling in colour.)

years later, Judi Bowker starred in Brother Sun, Sister Moon. *I wanted to be discovered, dammit, to be shot to international stardom with just one movie! But in reality, I've always had a careful nature and instead of going to drama school to train, I went to university and emerged clutching my B.A. Hons in Drama and Theatre Arts, but no nearer to being hailed by the world's press as 'Most Promising Newcomer'. I wasn't likely to be the next Susan George since I wasn't even the right sex to be a sex-kitten.*

My first priority, therefore, was to rectify that particular state of affairs. However, changing from male to female is no overnight job, I can assure you. It's not like moving into a deluxe, fully furnished condominium; it's more like buying a delapidated old house and spending years renovating it. (The result may not be to everybody's taste, but it suits me.)

My chances of earning a living in the theatre during that time would have been nil. I had not yet been living as a woman long enough to be able to relax and convincingly portray another female character on stage — I was still too busy discovering myself. But meanwhile I had to earn a living somehow. Several prospective employers proved unsympathetic once they knew the full facts. The civil service, on the other hand, informed me it did not discriminate on grounds of sex (or colour) and since my qualifications were more than adequate, my change of gender would not preclude me from joining its ranks. I did so willingly.

My twenties taught me the virtue of patience. No longer was I desperate for recognition. What I wanted more than anything was to keep my head down for the time being. But I still had an unshakeable faith that sometime in the future I would emerge from my self-imposed cocoon to dazzle the public at large. Friends suggested that I should join an amateur theatre group in order to keep my hand in. I recoiled in horror. Join an amateur group? Moi? I was not an amateur, I reminded them sternly: I had a degree in the subject and I would either tread the boards as a professional or not at all. In fact, until I started singing jazz in 1981, I made only three exceptions to that rule.

The first was a John Cage Happening at the Roundhouse shortly after I left university. It was organised by one of my ex-tutors. I sat in an ox-cart and played the cello for exactly 6¼ minutes, then wandered about for 52 minutes 'just being' before climbing on to a platform and singing 'Help Me Make It Through The Night' over and over again during the climax of the piece. 'Help Me Make It

Above: Adèle in her Cleo Laine phase wearing her plastic, post-modern, Nancy-Cunard-eat-your-heart-out bangles. (No wonder Sunderland went berserk.)

Through The Show' would have been more appropriate.

I am quite proud of the second occasion. After leaving university I worked in the accounts department of the Midland Red Omnibus Company, which was pretty ludicrous since I still use my fingers to add up. There I met a girl called Jenny Ann Morris who played the piano part time. We put together our talents, such as they were, and our initials to form Amajam, a Cabaret Duo. Well, it was either that or Jamama. Apart from a talent competition at West Bromwich in which we came last and a disastrous audition for New Faces (oh, how I wept when my pal from university, Victoria Wood, won it, and my tears weren't altogether tears of joy), we did have one night of glory. Somehow, we bluffed our way into being the sole entertainment at the Sunderland Arts Centre one evening in March 1974.

I must say they did us proud, decorating the room with thirties prints, pot plants and a paper parrot in a cage. The room was packed, mostly with students from the local art college who turned up in full thirties regalia. I had a voice like a foghorn in those days with no upper register at all. I was vastly overweight too as the doctors were having fun experimenting on me with different drugs. My hair was set in an attractive orange Afro style (I was going through my Cleo Laine phase). The piano was hopelessly out of tune and the sustaining pedal was broken. All in all, things did not bode well for Amajam and yet against all odds we triumphed. My rewrites of Porter, Kern and Berlin (sacrilege!) were rapturously received. At the end of the evening, the handsomest boy in the audience asked me to autograph a five pound note and I left the stage feeling like Ella Fitzgerald and Raquel Welch rolled into one. Well, I was big enough for two people. Shortly afterwards, Amajam disbanded. Other arts centres didn't seem to feel the same way about us as Sunderland had.

My third appearance on any stage was a playreading I did for the Writers' Co-operative. I returned to the scene of my earlier triumph, the Roundhouse, to star, for one night only, as the eponymous heroine in a charming piece with a message entitled Gregor Samsa is Alive and Well and Living With Jemima Puddleduck *— Kafka meets Beatrix Potter. My scream of fury when I discovered my beetle swain in flagrante delicto with Melanie Dormouse shook the Roundhouse to its very foundations.*

This last magical night in the theatre took place shortly before I became a TOPS advisor. After that, I contented myself with wearing colourful clothes and singing at parties. If I was drunk enough, I could pretend that the raucous sounds I was making were just like Billie Holiday. After all, I'd done my fair share of suffering too over the years and I knew it would all be worthwhile soon — very soon . . .

Nikki Kaye and Marilyn in A Slice of Life *— note Marilyn's uncharacteristically gormless expression.*

CHAPTER THREE

A SLICE OF LIFE

A year passed and Marilyn, Lizzie and I all went our separate ways. Then in about May 1981 I was asked by a girl called Sarah whom I knew slightly to direct and appear in a one-act cabaret style fringe show that she was producing that September at the now defunct York and Albany Theatre Club in Camden Town. Songs were to be supplied by one Suzy Sherling and the bill was to be shared with another one-act written by Nikki Kaye who would appear in both shows.

About five weeks before the opening date we all met up at my flat to start work. Sarah arrived ready for work in a voluminous fun-fur and enormous dark glasses: I don't know who was more nervous, her or me. She took command instantly and filled the airwaves for some three hours informing us about schedules, deadlines, posters, designers, printing costs, publicity campaigns and goodness knows what. It was terribly impressive, but there was something missing. Eventually she paused for half a second and, sensing my chance, I ventured what seemed to be a foolish question.

'Have you got a script we can read?'

It was as though a new recruit to the ranks had asked Monty for the loan of a few bullets.

Sarah looked at me quizzically.

'Oh no!' she replied. 'We'll devise it as we go.'

'Aah,' I said, guardedly. Devising as we went seemed like taking climbing lessons half-way up Everest. 'Any idea of what the script will contain?'

'Oh,' said Sarah, 'a collection of women's poetry, some political tracts and songs from Suzy.'

I wasn't encouraged. Coming as I do from the non-Stanislavsky school of theatre where character interpretation begins and ends with how much you flash your eyes and show your teeth, I found the idea of an evening of women's poetry and political tracts almost worse than going out for dinner with John Denver. However, I didn't want to appear too superficial, so I suggested that we listen to Suzy's songs.

Suzy went to the piano. I didn't quite know what to think of her: she was extremely quiet and hadn't said much other than 'Hello' and 'White, no sugar' in several hours. She sat down and fiddled nervously with endless bits of paper. Eventually she plucked up courage and sang to us. She needn't have worried; her songs were lovely – quirky, heartbreaking lyrics with wistful airs that rambled

Above: Lizzie as The Divine Marlene in the blonde wig that Marilyn wore in Charley's Aunt *and wearing a floral blouse that Dillie made and regretted.*

unexpectedly round the keys in a way my stodgy old professor would have abhorred. I was much encouraged – I knew the music would be good.

The next day Sarah arrived waving a thick file. I had thrown down the gauntlet and, like me, she was a woman to whom gauntlets were as matchwood to muscle men.

'Here's the script!' she cried. 'I've been up all night collating it!'

I looked through it quickly. As promised, it was women's poetry and political tracts interspersed with Suzy's songs. I no longer have the original script but I can remember it clearly. A typical section ran roughly thus: –

PERSON A   *Women make up 52% of the world's population and yet*
they own only 1% of the property.

PERSON B   *I put on the coffee pot.*
I look out over the sill.
Thoughts drift.
And collide.
I see the child.
My child.
And yet not mine.
I take off the coffee pot.

PERSON A   *52% of women never have an orgasm. 40% of those*
remaining only ever have clitoral orgasms. The other
5% claim to have vaginal orgasms once a fortnight
and even then only when there's an 'R' in the month.

PERSON B   *It is time*
To put on the coffee pot
Once again.
And dream of what lies
Beyond the sill.

PERSON A   *In Russia, women tractor drivers are found to be*
more likely to experience vaginal orgasm — 47%
claim to experience them at a frequency of two per
week, rising to a maximum of 3.2 per day during the
Warsaw Pact Manoeuvres.

PERSON B   *I take off the coffee pot.*
(Suzy sings song about love)

It was all good solid stuff and a great read, but not terribly theatrical, and I somehow doubted that my participation would either add anything substantial to the show or have the folk around Camden responding with the necessary unbridled enthusiasm.

I voiced my doubts about the possibilities of success with such a show. Sarah, breezy as March, assured me that I would undoubtedly contribute some great comedy sketches, and the whole thing would be a triumph. I demurred, feeling that my style was altogether too lowbrow for such an educational entertainment. Then I suddenly remembered a short play I had written some years before while going off my trolley temping in a Spanish bank in the City. I was simply there as fleshly evidence of status, and there was damn all to do other than to revolutionise the filing system. This had limited attractions as a way of passing the hours, so I wrote a comedy instead. It was based on my other life as a Career Temp on the Hilsea Trading Estate at Portsmouth.

I produced the script rather diffidently from the depths of a trunk and we read it aloud. Suzy and Nikki were hysterical with laughter after a couple of minutes and Sarah sat nodding delightedly.

'Yes, this is great!' she said, brimming with enthusiasm. 'With Suzy's songs and a few other bits . . . mmm . . . I'll take it home with me tonight and work on it.'

Sarah arrived the next day looking radiant despite the fact that she'd been up all night (again!) making alterations, and handed me the revised text with an air of nervous confidence.

I looked. I saw. I reeled. I felt a wave of artistic temperament sweeping over me. To my absolute horror, I saw that she had literally taken a pair of scissors and cut my precious first oeuvre, my baby, into ribbons and, forgetting that it was the only copy, had sellotaped the remaining shreds of my hopeful masterpiece on to all her pieces of poetry, tracts and statistics, as well as Suzy's songs.

A typical passage now ran thus:

(The scene is the typing pool:
Characters — MARLENE and MRS BOSTOCK who hold sway
therein.)

MARLENE	*We 'ad a letter from my Dad this mornin'.*
MRS BOSTOCK	*Ooh. Still in Australia then, is he?*
MARLENE	*Mmm.*
MRS BOSTOCK	*Still with that girl then, is he?*
MARLENE	*Yeah.*
MRS BOSTOCK	*Oooh. Shame. She was ever so young, wasn't she?*

MARLENE   (Bitterly) Nineteen.

MRS BOSTOCK   Oooh. Shaaame. What was her name then?

MARLENE   Marge. He never could afford the real thing.

MRS BOSTOCK   In South America, female hemp pickers do 98%
                 of the work, own only .0004% of the property,
                 and experience orgasms one in every three
                 Christmasses.

MARLENE   It is time
                 To brew the coffee once more.

                 (Suzy sings 'Tune into the Lord')

Suffice it to say that it was not a happy combination. Besides which,
it would have run at approximately three and a half hours and taken
at a gallop at that.

However, Sarah had been offered a job which meant she'd have
to start work immediately. She could not then be involved 100% in
the production. Having set the whole thing up though she was
understandably reluctant to let go of the reins completely, and for a
few days would arrive at odd times and redirect what we'd done.
This was no way to work, so for the benefit of all involved, Nikki
and I effected a putsch and ousted a miserable Sarah. It was a bit
unkind, but it was the best thing in the circumstances.

Marilyn had by this time got involved, and so she, Nikki, Suzy and
I got to work on the script after I had reconstituted the play. Suzy
sang us almost every song she'd ever written, the other two made
suggestions for plot and character development, and I spent long
nights manically typing up new scenes.

Casting was as follows: I was a natural for Beryl Bostock,
frustrated dragon of the typing pool and hopelessly in love with
Derek Dunwoody, the office lech who was played by an old drama
school friend, Noel Diacono. Poor Beryl: she was an unloved and
unlovely creature. Nikki was to play Karen, the hapless sociology
student temping in her vacation, and current object of Mr Dunwoody's insatiable lust and therefore Beryl's undying hatred. Marilyn
took the part of Elaine, the incredibly dim-witted and down-trodden
office junior who's been knocked up by Mr Dunwoody in the
stationery cupboard at the Christmas party. Lizzie Richardson was
drafted in as Marlene, Sex Queen of the Spare Parts Factory,
Hilsea's own Marilyn Monroe, beloved of Terry the Body Builder (a
near mythical figure who never appears) and unattainable to the
lecherous worm Dunwoody.

In the end, the play was about how terrible women can be to one another, and yet so supportive when the need arises (even Beryl comes good in the end). So it did have a message after all! Perhaps it was a little naïve, but there was a ring of truth that, with some fine comic moments, made it a very minor (but to me, major) success.

Nica Burns, she of Crewe, was asked to choreograph the songs and ended up directing the whole show, doing a great job. The cast was universally excellent and Marilyn's performance a tour de force of gormlessness. She inadvertently picked the title: she was talking about it to Sarah and said 'It's like a slice of life with footnotes,' the footnotes being the songs, and I pounced upon it as the ideal title.

We named the company 'Efemera'. I had been much struck when typing for my wildlife photographer by the life-cycle of the mayfly (*Ephemera* in Latin) which emerges at dawn from its chrysalis, iridescent lace wings a-shimmer, only to mate, lay its eggs and pop its clogs in the pond that same evening without having eaten a single morsel of lunch. Given the ad hoc nature of the operation, I felt that this would be a one-off affair, and so we adopted the name and changed the 'ph' to 'f' to add the right feminist touch.

We ran for two weeks at the York and Albany, and in spite of the *Time Out* strike which was on at the time and meant that nobody in London knew where anything at all fringish was on, it attracted good crowds. Then on the last night, a rummy looking cove came up and introduced himself as Dan Crawford, doyen of the King's Head in Islington.

'Er, hi,' he said, speaking in a clipped drawl that floated somewhere between JFK and Heathrow. 'I really liked your . . . um, show, and . . . was wondering if you'd . . . uhm, be interested in doing the show at . . . hrmm, the King's Head?'

It can therefore honestly be said that, thanks to Sarah, my first play had a London transfer, and while it wasn't quite *She Stoops to Conquer*, it was a daisy and I'm more fond of it than of anything else I've ever done, and it established Lizzie, Marilyn and me as the trio.

In the last week at Islington, the atmosphere suddenly turned sour. Lizzie had to leave as she got a proper job and we discussed getting a replacement. Nica seemed to be the obvious choice; she knew it inside out and would have been very funny, especially in a blonde wig. She was extremely reluctant, but eventually agreed to do it provided we discussed it amongst ourselves.

Like a good collective, the cast debated it, and it seemed there was only one drawback: Nica's voice which, hard to credit, is even more tuneless than mine. She had appeared in a number of musicals up and down the land but more on the strength of her dancing and her killing rendition of 'Hernando's Hideaway' as an audition piece

which was so outrageous that you quickly forgot about the voice. The same voice tackling Suzy's sensitive ballads was not quite so acceptable.

We decided that she could play the part provided the songs were rearranged: I would sing them, and she would interpret them through her dancing.

I was deputed to notify Nica of our decision.

'Ah, Nica!' I said. 'I've had a chat with the cast.'

'Oh, right,' she said. 'What's the verdict?'

'Good news and bad news,' said I, confident of my tact. 'The good news is that we all think you should definitely do it.'

'Oh, okay,' she said.

'The bad news is that we all think (note that I was underlining the collective decision to exonerate myself from any personal responsibility) you shouldn't sing the songs.'

'Why not?'

I failed to notice the rapid blinking and the brimming tears.

'Oh, because you can't sing!' In with both feet.

We barely spoke for two years. In one fell swoop I had shattered her most cherished illusion, and humiliated her when she hadn't even wanted to do the part in the first place. Nowadays when she rubbishes some new song of mine, as she occasionally does, I bite my tongue and remember how mean I was.

Above: Dillie (in another appealing guise) as Mrs. Bostock yearning for a very blurred Mr. Dunwoody (Noël Diacono). SORRY NOËL - IT WAS THE ONLY PHOTO I HAD OF YOU.

THE PIRATES OF PENZANCE

Once again Marilyn, Lizzie and I went out separate ways to do proper jobs and my hopes of ever getting a permanent trio together were as far away as ever. We met fairly regularly to do auditions. At least, Marilyn and Lizzie did the auditions and I accompanied them. Pianists have all the best fun: they get to play for their friends' auditions and they get to play at parties when everyone begs them to play and nobody listens. Still, it saves having to flirt.

In November 1981, I got a call from Marilyn asking me to tinkle at yet another audition. She'd been asked to play Kate, one of the Major-General's daughters in the Dublin production of *The Pirates of Penzance*, and as Billy Whelan, the arranger, was visiting London, the producer wanted him to hear Marilyn's voice.

I was full of envy as my brother and sister-in-law live in Dublin and I still had a good number of college friends in Ireland. Besides which, I was suffering from the effects of a stupendously disastrous non-romance and would have done anything to flee the country for a few years. I had even applied to the Polish Embassy to go and study drama in Poland for two years, that's how desperate I was.

Marilyn and I hatched a plot for the audition whereby instead of her singing a solo for Billy, we'd sing a duet. After all, she had nothing to lose as she'd already been offered a part provided she could sing in tune and there was no chance of her blowing that. He would then be so moved and uplifted by the liquid gold that would come pouring from my throat that he'd ring up the producer there and then and say 'La Cutts is magnificent and, what's more, we've got to have Dillie Keane in the show! She's hot!!!'

So we sang for him, and gave him tea: not necessarily the right choice for an Irishman at around 6.00 pm, but he was very gracious about it. He was quite enthusiastic about the idea of having me in the cast (my voice was in better shape in those days) and said he'd put in a good word. I duly packed off an official snap and a curriculum vitae to the producer and said a few Novenas to St Jude the patron saint of hopeless cases. To no avail. The part I'd applied for, that of Ruth the Maid-of-all-Work (the alto), had gone to a leading actress in Dublin and there were no other vacancies. I was disconsolate. Marilyn and I had a farewell supper and she went off to the Emerald Isle.

I was sitting moodily in my flat some ten days later feeling that the world was my onion when I got a call from Dublin. It was St Jude turning up trumps. Someone had dropped out of the production with a nasty case of nodules (oh Heavenly Nodules!) and the cry went up – 'Send for Dillie Keane!' Would I be interested, they asked, in taking a part although it was only in the chorus? Would I be interested in singing Gilbert's incomparable lyrics and Sullivan's glorious tunes for two hours a night, eight performances a week? I had my case packed and was on the plane before you could say 'I am the very Model of a Modern Major-General'.

The show was a smash hit. People who'd seen the original Broadway version with Linda Ronstadt said it was the better of the two, and those who ultimately saw all three productions (i.e. the London one as well) said that it was the best of the lot. The choreographer (Mavis Ascott) and director (Patrick Mason) were both English and this, coupled with the innate sense of anarchy in the Irish and their empathy with G & S for its brilliant wordiness and astonishing tunefulness made for a dynamite combination.

The most marvellous thing for me was that I discovered my 'clown'. We'd done clown classes at drama school and I had searched vainly in my innermost parts for the clown I was assured lay hidden inside everyone. I frankly doubted its existence by the end of a couple of fruitless terms which I spent capering about like a dingbat, and gave up the search after finding nothing other than a few obsessions which I'd prefer not to reveal here. Awful self-indulgent theatrical hogwash, I thought.

I was wrong.

Discovering one's clown is the greatest thing that can happen to an actor because it's so – and I hate to use this word because it sounds so pretentious but I have no alternative – liberating. It's like suddenly being able to let free the real person inside you – the person who at a polite gathering rips off her knickers and shouts 'Whoopee!'; the person who doesn't give a damn whether her lipstick matches her nail polish or if she can talk intelligently about the Third World; the person who is defeated, humiliated, resourceful, cowardly, cunning, unhappy. The clown is the anarchist inside who reveals and uses all those traits which he or she may be secretly fond of but which might be deemed socially unacceptable. Most importantly, the clown *is* the person, or an extension of the person.

Being a clown isn't just a matter of frolicking around in baggy clothes with a sad white face. In the case of circus clowns, each face is quite different down to the finest detail. They all have their own way of walking, moving, dressing, being, and whether boisterous or inclined to melancholy, the clown's signature and copyright trademark is the face. Each has his own style and no two faces are the same. Many male performers discover their clown – Max Wall, Charlie Chaplin and Nigel Planer being prime examples – but women less so. (Joyce Grenfell and Victoria Wood are wonderful exceptions.) This I'm sure is because women are brought up to look pretty at all times. It's a legacy left to us from the days when women were women and men were gods.

The glossy magazines further perpetuate the myth of the ideal woman, only now she has to reach new heights of perfection. The ideal woman windsurfs, paraglides, sunbathes in the nude, cooks in a wok, counts kilojoules instead of calories, and has a wonderful way with tradescantia. She wears gloriously chic little outfits that turn out to be second hand numbers thrown together as if by magic. She always takes her make-up off at night to keep wrinkles at bay, having drunk Perrier all evening. She is always, always decorative and yet runs a successful business and has read every book by Frederic Forsyth and Erica Jong. She is always sexy, desirable, scented, and has multiple orgasms at the drop of a hemline. She is, in short, pure Conran.

An impossible and, to me, undesirable way to be. Jolly tiring, to say the least. And for many actresses it affects the ability to perform. With great willingness they'll out on rags and false warts and play the part of a destitute, but that's because they're obviously being 'someone else'. Ask them to appear as themselves and voluntarily make eejits of themselves and you have a problem. They simply can't send themselves up – it's too much against the grain. The desperate, consuming need to look attractive is much more powerful than the need to be a good performer.

And there you have the key to being a clown; the clown takes those aspects of herself which she finds most ludicrous (and often most heart-breakingly recognisable to the audience) and emphasises them as a cartoonist would a prominent nose. It's as if the concentrated essence of one person were used to create another, and that other turns out to be your long-lost twin.

A clown is, however, not the same thing as a comic actor. Take Tony Hancock and Peter Sellers for instance. Both have impeccable comic timing, but Hancock is always Hancock. Peter Sellers on the other hand is a million different things: an inept French detective, an urbane Indian doctor, a mad Chinaman: the list is endless. The difference between them is that where Peter Sellers puts on masks and dazzles us with his characterisations and his observations of the foibles of the human race, Hancock always reveals himself, and it is Hancock who breaks our hearts. Of course, Inspector Clouseau did become Sellers' clown as the character became more and more absurd and ludicrously inept, and it is interesting that he is best

loved and remembered for the Pink Panther films: after all, there is something of Clouseau in most of us – the absurdly dignified, conscientious dunderhead with grand ambitions and a sneaking terror that he might just be completely out of his depth.

I keep talking about men, and it's very difficult not to because women clowns are rare, even though we seem to be entering a golden age of women comedians. There are a few more around now: besides the incomparable Victoria Wood, there are Su Pollard, Dawn French and Jennifer Saunders, but the temptation to go for the lip gloss and earn the mega-bucks is strong.

And despite the fact that there is a whole new generation of women comedians coming up, there is still a great deal of resistance on the part of the media to women clowns. It seems that women are seen as losing their mystique (whatever that is) the moment they stray from the accepted bounds of feminine humour. They can be perky, like Felicity Kendal, or horsey, like Penelope Keith, but they can't be undignified: as soon as Pamela Stephenson started behaving in a way incompatible with her magazine cover image, she was heavily criticised.

One night in Dublin I was summoned to the bar after the show. A party of six ladies had seen it and wanted to meet me to tell me how much they had enjoyed my performance. They greeted me with blank surprise.

Above: Marilyn, another chorine, and Dillie as her clown in the dressing room.

Inset: Some time after Marilyn left for the bright lights of the West End, the show was re-reviewed in the Irish Times *(Dr. David Nowlan)*

'Are youze de wan wi' da plaits and glasses?' asked one lady suspiciously.

'Yes,' I said.

'Ye were carryin' a book, were ya?' asked another, apparently mystified.

'Yes, that was me.' I wondered what was so amazing. Admittedly I did look pretty different, but not *that* different.

'Do that thing wit' yer eyes!' commanded another in search of hard proof. Obliging to the last, I rolled one eye wildly, a talent that my nephew Dominic envies wildly. The whole group of ladies broke out in hysterical laughter.

'It is her, it is her!' they said to one another. 'Jeez,' they said to me, 'we thought ye were a man. We thought it was definitely a man got up to amuse us, like. Ah, you're the image of Phil Silvers, the image of him.'

The inference being, perhaps, that no woman would deliberately make herself up to be that hideous? And yet being compared to Phil Silvers was the greatest compliment I ever had in my life.

Thanks, then, mainly to Mavis the choreographer, who really let me reinterpret all her moves in my own fashion and indeed encouraged us all to use our own personalities as outlandishly as possible while leaping about in the chorus, I suddenly realised that I'd got to the top of the mountain without even noticing the climb. The wardrobe department unwittingly helped by giving me a frightful wig that made me look like Charles I and the only thing to do was plait it . . . and put wire in the plaits to make them stick out . . . After that came horn-rimmed specs, huge freckles, serpentine eyebrows and tiny red lips that looked sphincterish rather than labial. Gradually, another person began to emerge, a plain, prim and puckish bookworm in a state of permanent high dudgeon.

Marilyn left the show about half way through (it ran for about seven months which in a city the size of Dublin is phenomenal). She got homesick for London as did I for the first while. (Then I got so fond of Dublin again that I've been homesick for it ever since I left – daft.) So when an offer came through for her to go to the West End and do *Design for Living* with Maria Aitken, she was off and into the distance like Red Rum. I missed her: we worked well together.

I did 195 performances of *Pirates* and that made an awful lot of free days to fill. So in order to occupy my time usefully, I took up gardening which is of interest to no-one but myself, and also decided to write a play. My sister-in-law Noreen had alerted me to a notice in the *Irish Times* announcing a Women's Playwriting Competition in conjunction with the Dublin Theatre Festival. Full of confidence after my London Transfer, I decided to enter. Dublin being a very small city, I knew two of the judges, so entered my oeuvre under a friend's name. She was most pleasantly surprised to hear that her entry had been short-listed as a possible winner.

Now it may seem as though I have been blowing my own trumpet with my glowing recollections of *Pirates* and *A Slice of Life*. Well, the moment has come for me to do the reverse (suck my own trumpet?), for the play was the beastliest bit of tosh ever to disgrace clean white paper. Luckily, it didn't win or even come second as then it would have automatically merited a production at the Abbey and my name would have been mud for ever. It came in the last four though, and about eighteen months later got put on by a Dublin production company who had faith in it and toured it to lucky Tralee, Cork, Sligo and the armpit of the western world, Limerick. Limerick deserved it – what's more, they thought it was the finest new play to come to Limerick in many a long year. They would. The other towns were more sagacious and dismissed it for the infernal rubbish that it was.

It was called *Boat People* and my cheeks burn every time I think about it. I've still not got over the embarrassment of having to face the cast. It might have stood more of a chance if I could have attended rehearsals and done rewrites, but I was up to my oxthers in FA by then and so could do nothing to alleviate the actors' hopeless situation. At least they were paid to be in it: many innocent Irish folk paid to see it.

By curious coincidence, Tralee, where it was premiered, was my mother's home town and *Boat People* opened on the same night that J. B. Keane's (no relation) last play opened in Listowel in the same county of Kerry. My aunt, who still lives in Tralee, came to see *Boat People* with me.

'God Almighty!' she exclaimed. 'Did you write all that bloody rubbish?'

Pirates closed in about August 1982, and I trailed slowly back to London, completely at a loss as to what to do next. *Boat People* was to get a public airing in a series of women's play readings a couple of months later (which then got put off for a few more months) and I wanted to be around for that, which meant not putting myself on the job marketplace. I couldn't face going back to straight acting again after the glorious anarchy of *Pirates*: going the rounds of auditions and enduring all the humiliation that that involved: and, in the event of getting a job, hauling my battered suitcase from rep to rep, and for what? To spout other people's lines?

I also felt desolate without my clown: it was like being bereaved of my best friend or losing a limb. One night I was so acutely lonely that I had to struggle with myself not to put on the make-up and wig again, just to be able to see her. I hit an all-time low.

I began to explore the possibility of going to France to study mime, and Poland reared its head again as a possibility. Well, I wasn't going to be a playwright, that much was obvious. In the meantime, I very slowly began to write some more songs. This time they were pithier and better constructed – it must have been all that G & S rubbing off on me.

Marilyn and Lizzie were both appearing in the West End, being glamorous actresses. *Design for Living* threatened to run and run, swallowing Marilyn up for ever, and Lizzie was playing all the women in *Private Dick* opposite Robert Powell. I managed to galvanise them into doing some daytime rehearsals and we met fairly often to work on the three part harmony arrangements of the songs I'd written. They sounded lovely, so I decided it was time to test the water and when a friend told me about a new fringe venue in Chelsea that was looking for acts to put on at lunchtime on Sundays, I gave them a ring and got us a gig that October. (Well, Sunday lunchtime was virtually the only time the others were ever free.) It was inaptly called 'The Hollywood Bar', and the so-called 'theatre' was run by a very odd fish called Peter who fancied himself as an up-and-coming mega-cheese in the strange demi-monde of alternative theatre.

We were completely stuck for a name. The joke of 'Shame' had worn thin, so we toyed with various ideas. 'The Doxies' and 'The Frockettes' were front runners, I recall with a blush, and 'Efemera' was still in the running. I suggested 'Muddle' as the consonants matched our initials – M, D, and L – but Marilyn said witheringly that in that case, 'Mould' would be more suitable. Someone mooted 'Sluts with Brains' due to an unrepeatable incident between myself and a drummer in Dublin, but it had altogether the wrong connotations. We returned unhappily to 'Shame' and I was deputed to ring the Hollywood Bar and inform the organisers so they could fix up some publicity, whereupon they immediately tried to cancel the gig.

We had an awful row that lasted two days and which I won. However, the question of the name slipped out of focus a little and we were billed as 'The Dillie Keane Trio', probably as revenge. As Marilyn said in a steely voice when she saw it, it made us sound like a fifties swing combo featuring me on keyboards, Lizzie on tenor sax, and herself on tea-chest and broom handle.

The gig was a great success, and many friends turned up and were extremely encouraging about the possibilities of the group. This was all very well, but with the other two in constant employment, it could only go nowhere fast. It was extremely frustrating.

The rest of 1982 passed uneventfully for me. I saw Marilyn take over Maria Aitken's part in *Design for Living* (she had been her understudy as well as having had a part of her own) and jolly good she was too. But then, as she herself said, it was easy to be good when you got to kiss both Gary Bond and Ian Ogilvy. I returned to my career at the piano and typewriter keyboards, and wondered what to do with my life; I had passed the thirty mark the previous May and was beginning to feel that time was no longer on my side.

Then something really momentous happened – I went to a New Year's Eve Party.

I had given my solemn promise to Pattie Coldwell (ex-Crewet) that I would go up to the bash being given in her old flat in Didsbury. Frankly, I was cursing. Trekking up by train to Manchester on a cold December night, even if it was going to be January in the morning, did not tempt me. I felt more like going to bed with an apple and a good book. But a promise is a promise, so when I had spent several hours trying vainly to get through to British Rail to find out the times of the trains, I was overwhelmed by a mood of enraged extravagance and hired a car – a rash move for someone in an advanced state of penury. These are fine details you may find of little interest. But if I hadn't made the effort and gone to the party, I wouldn't have met the producer of *Start the Week*, the Radio 4 programme that graces our airwaves every Monday morning. And if I hadn't hired a car, I couldn't have given her a lift home the next day and we would probably never again have had the opportunity to talk for five hours at a stretch. And Pattie would have been extremely disappointed that all her plans had gone for nothing, because of course the meeting was an elaborate set-up. (It has to be said that Fascinating Aïda's progress has often been due to the machinations of generous and faithful friends, and Pattie is top of the list.)

The party itself was as hairy as a body could desire with all the elements a really steamy Hogmanay requires: gate-crashers, tears, drama, sex and drugs and rock 'n' roll, people being sick in the garden – it was brilliant. And six o'clock in the morning found me *au dehors de mon arbre* and at last acquiescing with Pattie's urgent requests to sing my songs to the last of the drunken revellers whilst accompanying myself on her minuscule electric keyboard. In the next room was Jenny Danks, the aforementioned producer, who'd by then given in to exhaustion. In her hypnogoguic state she dimly heard the waves of laughter, and on the way home the next day asked me all about my songs, how long I'd been writing, and did I intend to go on writing. When we arrived in London, she took my telephone number and said she'd give me a ring about doing something for the programme. I thought nothing of it as I've learned through my life never to believe any promises or offers until I've got the duty free in my hands.

A few days later she called me. Would I do a song for the next edition of *Start the Week*? I nearly dropped the telephone. 'Yes!' I said quickly before I had time to change my mind. The allotted subject was recreation, as this was to be the main theme of the programme. 'Thank God,' I thought, as I already had most of 'The Jogging Song' written. So it was finished off hurriedly and given to the world for the first time that January.

The world was generally unmoved, but I was deluged with offers from the rest of the media. Well, two. The first was from TVAM. I did a couple of songs for them, but it was extremely frustrating because they kept postponing the dates of transmission and so all my loyal family and friends who'd got up at the ungodly hour of 6.30 to watch two and a half hours of visual muesli were extremely irked when they realised they'd have to do it again the following Saturday.

My second offer came from Michael Ember, producer of *Stop the Week* which is the sister programme to *Start the Week* and goes out on Saturday evenings. It's the kind of programme you either love or loathe – I've always been a big fan so when Michael rang to offer me the chance of doing a couple of shows, I was stricken with abject terror and said no. The thought of my footling ditties interrupting Robert Robinson and Co.'s fascinatingly mordant conversation was too overwhelming for lyrics. Then I had second thoughts and cursed myself for a frightful gombeen, and rang Michael back.

'I'm so glad you've decided to do it,' he said in a disarming middle European accent. 'But I wonder, perhaps . . . you see, after a five way conversation, to have, ah, just one voice and one instrument sound a little thin. Do you know any other musicians who could play with you – a drummer or a guitarist perhaps?'

Guitarist I knew none, and I'd left all the drummers I knew back in Dublin.

'I don't know any musicians, Michael,' I said worriedly, thinking that this might stop me getting the gig. Suddenly I thought of Marilyn and Lizzie. 'I've got a couple of girlfriends that I sing with. Would that do?'

'Yes, I think that would be fine,' he said. 'Shall we try two dates in March and see how they go?'

It was our first booking.

CHAPTER FIVE

SUPER OLGA

or

How We Got The Name Fascinating Aïda

(A Short Play in Four Scenes)

or

Positively The Last Time I Ever Tell This Bloody Story

SCENE ONE

It is January 1983, a hot, sultry night in Mexico City.
The setting is a hotel lounge: various armchairs, sofas, tables etc. and waiters passing through. A poster on the wall screams 'SUPER OLGA 1983!! IN CABARET AT THE HILTON HOTEL!'
   MICHAEL FITZGERALD, an actor known as Fitz (see Chapter One — Crewe), paces restlessly around the room. Something seems to be troubling him.

FITZ   (*Muttering to himself*) To be, or not to be, that is the riddle . . . no, that's not right . . . to sleep, perchance to snooze . . . ay, there's the club . . .

(MARTHA enters. She is a plump, energetic American girl and is FITZ's travelling companion in Mexico. She greets FITZ enthusiastically.)

MARTHA   Hiya, Fitzy Baby! How ya doin'?

FITZ   Oh God, oh God, how weary, stale, flat and unprofitable seem to me all the uses of this world.

MARTHA   Nice hotel, huh?

FITZ   Fie, 'tis an unweeded garden . . .

MARTHA   That's too bad! My room's a palace! Ain't your bed comfortable?

FITZ   Is this a nagger that I see before me?

MARTHA   Say, is sump'n' gettin' ya down, Fitzy? Aw, whaddya say we go out, take in a few sights, look around ol' Mexico City?

FITZ   Tomorrow, and tomorrow, and tomorrow . . .

MARTHA   Hey, has somebody been botherin' you, boss? I'll fix 'em for ya.

FITZ   Words, words, words . . .

MARTHA   Gee, I never seen you so bad, boss. Youze lookin' sore as a buzzard's ass in a sandstorm.

FITZ   I look like an old peeled wall — no, that's not right: I am a seagull . . .

MARTHA   Hey, I got just da thing for youze dat'll bring da roses back to ya cheeks. Whaddya say we go see a show, 'n' feast our peepers on some dancin' goils?

FITZ   (*Beginning to look interested*) The play's the thing, and all the world's a cabaret venue . . .

MARTHA   I knew dat 'ud wake ya up. How's about goin' to see Fascinatin' Aïda, or whatever her name is.

FITZ   (*Now completely roused from his torpor*) Fascinating who?

MARTHA   Fascinatin' Aïda. Dat hotsy-totsy poopsie who's appearin' at da Hilton Hotel. I seen her advoitisements all over da place.

FITZ   Do you mean Super Olga?

MARTHA   Fascinatin' Aïda, Super Olga . . . what's the difference? She sure does look like your type of goil, boss. (*Noticing the poster on the wall*) Hey, look, she's over dere on da wall. (*Reads*) 'Super Olga in her fabulous new show for 1983, in Cabaret at da Hilton Hotel Penthouse Restaurant, appearin' nightly Monday to Saturday at eight thoity p.m.'

FITZ   Eight thirty? But it's already a quarter past . . . We'd better call a cab!

MARTHA   Time's wingèd heels, huh?

FITZ   Pardon? Come on, we'll be late!

MARTHA   Okey dokey, boss.

FITZ   By the way, how did you get the name Fascinating Aïda out of Super Olga?

MARTHA   Gee, I dunno. Mus' be my background in grand opera playin' tricks on my subconscious, I guess.

FITZ   (*Musingly*) Fascinating Aïda . . . ? Mmm, I have a friend who should call herself Fascinating Aïda.

MARTHA   Yeah? Gee, she sho' does sound like an unfoitunate dame. (*She starts to go*)

FITZ   (*As he goes*) Gallop apace, ye fiery footed steeds, t'wards Olga's lodging . . .

END OF SCENE ONE

SCENE TWO

The Cabaret Room at the Hilton Hotel. The audience is packed — FITZ and MARTHA have been lucky to get seats at all. It seems that Super Olga is quite a heroine in Mexico.

Suddenly, the lights dim, and the band begins to play. The stage lights come up, and Olga herself comes on, surrounded by seven dancing boys.

For two hours, she entertains an enraptured audience. She dances, sings, cracks jokes, and even though her act is entirely in Spanish, FITZ and MARTHA sit enthralled along with the rest of the crowd. She dances with snakes. She takes all her clothes off and underneath her clothes are hundreds of tiny little mirrors covering her body which then become the focal point of a laser beam light show.

She makes dozens of entrances, each time in a costume more phantastique than the last. She comes on with the comedian, and they have bells tuned to different pitches tied to their extremities: they play tunes by shaking the bells in turn, and of course the top note is tied to her bosom.

Finally, she comes on in a very simple black dress and carrying a violin. She lifts the violin, places it underneath her chin and proceeds to play classical music absolutely beautifully.

As the house lights come back on at the end of the show, FITZ and MARTHA sit there, stunned. After a long pause, FITZ speaks.

FITZ   That is simply the best show I have ever seen in my life.

END OF SCENE TWO

SCENE THREE

Back in England, FITZ is visiting DILLIE after his Mexico holiday.

FITZ   Dillie, you've got to change your name to Fascinating Aïda.

DILLIE   Sorry?

FITZ   You've got to change your name to Fascinating Aïda.

DILLIE   Why?

FITZ   Because it would suit you. You *are* Fascinating Aïda. When I heard
              the name I knew it was you.

DILLIE   Don't be daft. Dillie Keane's bad enough. If I called myself Fascinating
              Aïda I'd never get another job. Why Fascinating Aïda anyhow?

FITZ   Well, when I was in Mexico, Martha . . . . (etc. etc.)

END OF SCENE THREE

SCENE FOUR

Two months later.

DILLIE's bedroom in her flat in West Hampstead. There is a piano against one wall, a bed and all the other things you'd expect in a bedroom. MARILYN and LIZZIE are sitting on the floor, surrounded by bits of paper, reference books, empty cups of coffee etc. They look extremely harassed. They are deep in the throes of writing their first Stop the Week *commission, and they only have thirty-six hours to write, arrange and rehearse the song.*
    Enter DILLIE. She is carrying a tray.

DILLIE   Coffee!

MARILYN   I better not. I've had eleven cups already.

LIZZIE   God, how are we ever supposed to write a song about *Who's Who* in just one day? It's impossible.

MARILYN   Maybe they've come up with another subject by now. I'll go and phone *Stop the Week*.

(MARILYN exits.)

LIZZIE   What rhymes with Who's Who?

DILLIE   Boo hoo.

LIZZIE   Thank you.

DILLIE   *(Looking in a copy of* Who's Who) Good heavens!

LIZZIE   What?

DILLIE   They haven't got Dolly Parton in here! What sort of a book is this anyhow?

LIZZIE   *(Appalled)* Gosh!

(MARILYN re-enters.)

DILLIE   Any luck?

LIZZIE   Did they have another subject?

MARILYN   *(Heavily)* Yes. Silk dressing-gowns.

LIZZIE   *(Incredulously)* Silk dressing-gowns?

MARILYN   Yes. Silk dressing-gowns.

DILLIE   I think we'd better stick with *Who's Who*.

MARILYN   Yes.

LIZZIE   Did you realise, Marilyn, that Dolly Parton isn't in *Who's Who*?

MARILYN   Really?

DILLIE   And neither is Mick Jagger.

LIZZIE   What do you have to do to get in it? I thought it was for famous people.

MARILYN   No, it's just a register of dignitaries in the Forestry Commission and the Ministry of Fish and Ag. It's all civil servants. *(Thoughtfully)*

Maybe we could do it from the point of view of someone like Dolly Parton?

DILLIE   You mean, like somebody really famous who's furious at not being in it?

MARILYN   Yes, absolutely.

LIZZIE   You could make it a Country and Western song.

DILLIE   Yes, at least that would be easy musically.

(*The phone rings.*)

DILLIE   I'll go.

(*Exit DILLIE.*)

MARILYN   (*Scribbling madly*) How about something like this: 'Well, I've just had a copy of *Who's Who* delivered and I searched there in vain for my entry . . .'

LIZZIE   Yes, let me just write that down, that's fine . . .

(*DILLIE re-enters with a long face.*)

MARILYN   Who was that?

DILLIE   It was *Stop the Week* again. They want to know what the name of the group is.

LIZZIE   Oh God, not again.

MARILYN   How soon do they need to know?

DILLIE   Twenty minutes. They're doing a trail for the programme.

MARILYN   Oh dear.

(*Long Pause.*)

DILLIE   How about the Frockettes?

(*Long Pause.*)

LIZZIE   The Doxies?

(*Long Pause.*)

DILLIE   Shame?

LIZZIE &   (*Together*)
MARILYN   Groan.

(*Long Pause. The atmosphere is getting positively Pinterish.*)

DILLIE   (*Lamely*) What about Fascinating Aïda?

LIZZIE &   (*Together: they have both heard Fitz's saga: non-committedly*) Oh,
MARILYN   all right.

DILLIE   Fine. I'll go and phone them up.

(*DILLIE exits.*)

LIZZIE   I've thought of a rhyme for 'entry'.

MARILYN   What?

LIZZIE   Gentry.

MARILYN   That's good. You could have something like: 'I searched there in vain
                 for my entry . . . blah di blah di blah di blah . . . I've been elbowed out
                 by the gentry.' Well, it's a start . . .

(*DILLIE re-enters.*)

DILLIE   Well, Fascinating Aïda it is.

MARILYN   Look, Dillie, I'm sorry, but I'm trying to concentrate.

DILLIE   Oh, all right. I think I'll just go down to the shop for a Mars Bar.
                 Anyone else want a Mars Bar? No? Fine. Fine.

SLOW FADE OUT ON SCENE FOUR

THE END

And if anyone ever asks me the origin of the name Fascinating Aïda again,
I'll scream.

THE BEST LAID PLANS . . .

Adèle again . . .

By 1980 I had served five years in the civil service and decided to leave. My faith in TOPS courses was not completely destroyed, though. My last act before I left was to put myself on one.

No charges of nepotism, please. I had to go through the same procedure as everybody else to be accepted. And so it came to pass that in September 1980 I began a year's study at Havering Technical College, Essex, at the end of which I would gain a Diploma for Personal Assistants (being one of four out of the thirteen on the course to do so) and be proficient in typing and Pitman shorthand. It was certainly a change of direction for me. For the past two years I had been on first-name terms with TOPS tutors. Now I was no longer an equal and had to call my tutors Miss or Mrs . . . (there weren't any Mses), just like the other girls, all of whom were much younger than I. It took me a few weeks to adjust. It was also a shock to the system to be studying once more after a gap of eight years. The last few months of the course were a very lean time but I passed with flying colours and the first stage of my plan had been completed.

What was the plan? Why, to return to the theatre of course. I say return, but in reality I'd never left it because, of course, I'd never been in it to begin with. No matter; that was how I thought. I had figured that I would need a skill to fall back on when I was 'resting' (ever the optimist, that's me) and being an ex-civil servant was no skill at all. Hence the secretarial course. After I graduated I began temping. Don't let anyone kid you it's glamorous or fun — it's neither. Where were the film producers, the record moguls, the fashion designers? Certainly not where I worked. I was invariably sent to magnitudinous financial institutions to work for men who were dry as dust. I wasn't allowed to do anything other than take dictation and type. 'Don't bother with that,' my temporary employer would grunt, 'Mavis (or whoever) will do it when she gets back next week.' I made endless cups of coffee and was reprimanded on more than one occasion for receiving (not making!) personal telephone calls. Most of these calls were from my agency, informing me of my next week's work or lack of it. Oh pity the poor deluded maiden. Not for her the pick of a thousand jobs weekly. She invariably spent Monday morning by the phone chewing her nails and wondering if she should cut her losses and run to the DHSS instead. I wouldn't have minded so much if I'd been going for auditions. But I had no agent and, what was worse, no Equity Card. As many of you will

Adèle recreates her rôle as a secretary. Note the expression of Job Satisfaction.

know (a favourite phrase of Emmy-Lee Brontë's, see p. 137) no card = no job and no job = no way of getting a card. This was a major flaw in my plan. Therefore, I reasoned, my next step was to set about gaining a card as soon as possible (or ℮ℓℴ as we say in shorthand). This would take time, though, and by now I was broke, so there was only one thing for it — get a permanent job.

It took a few interviews to find a job. I guess I couldn't disguise the fact that I didn't really want to be a secretary. However, Mr Sidney Lunt of IPC Magazines didn't seem to mind this. His wife had been an actress years ago and still sometimes wished she hadn't given it up. So he understood how I felt, but also believed I might find an outlet for my artistic ambitions within the world of publishing. I wouldn't find it with him, mind you, since he was in charge of catering for the 2,500 employees who toiled within the King's Reach Tower, but he could at least provide a way in for me. I liked Sid Lunt very much. No one could have been a kinder employer. I've yet to meet another secretary whose boss would make her a coffee or pour her a gin and tonic at 12.30 hours every day (well, most days). During the three years I was with him he never broke faith with his original promise to promote my interest within the organisation. The trouble was I had no interest. If I allowed myself to be drawn into the world of publishing I might well lose sight of my original goal — the theatre. So I stayed put, safe in the catering department. There was a problem though. I had very little to do. OK, so in the first few months I'd rearranged the office and weeded out the filing cabinet but after that, apart from a monthly accounts sheet, I had a lot of time on my hands.

I have to come clean here and confess that I'm a telephone addict. I've given up writing letters in favour of the immediacy of the telephone. I was in seventh heaven the day I bought an answering machine. If I wish I can dial my machine from the other side of the world and change my own message with the aid of my little bleeper. I don't, mind you, but I could if I wanted to. Anyway, poor Mr Lunt's telephone bills shot up and if it hadn't been that it was impossible to dial abroad they'd have been even higher. I'm also one of those people who cannot pretend to be busy when there is no work to do. So what was the point of getting to work on time, or only taking an hour for lunch when the alternative was to sit in my office twiddling my thumbs?

Mr Lunt was extremely long-suffering and was loath to replace me because at least my letters were first-rate and we had such great chats on a wide variety of topics. However, by the end of 1983 he'd had enough. So had I, really, but I was hooked on my monthly pay cheque. The memory of my year of penury as a student was still fresh in my mind. In November Mr Lunt suggested to me that either I become a perfect secretary with all that that entailed (i.e. meticulous time-keeping and no more personal telephone calls) or I leave and do what I'd been telling him for the past three years I wanted to do — act. I talked it over with my flatmate Stevan. Stevan Rimkus is a young blond Scottish actor who, with hair dyed black and a strong Belfast accent, chillingly portrayed the killer Crillie in Pat O'Connor's moving film Cal, *starring Helen Mirren and Jon Lynch. He pointed out that I hadn't enjoyed my job during the six months he'd known me and that that wasn't likely to change. Moreover, I was now 30 and should get a move on if I was going to become famous. After all, I'd have to look good in the photographs. Finally, he vowed that, since he'd made a few bob from the movie, while I was out of work he'd support me financially (he didn't!). On 1st December I gave in my notice at IPC. I hadn't been completely idle during those years, you see. I now had an Equity Card.*

TABOO

Spoken: We would never sing songs about things that would shock people, such as unwanted facial hair, stains, shpeech defectsh, or

Sung: Inviting a vegan to a barbecue
Meeting Joan Collins and saying 'Joan Who?'
Yelling 'Titanic' on the Q.E.2.
It's taboo it's taboo it's taboo:

When you're kissing it's having bad breath
With your granny, talking 'bout death,
If you're an actor, it's quoting 'Macb. . . .'
It's taboo it's taboo it's taboo.

Taboo is doing things that you shouldn't oughta
Like blessing Ian Paisley with holy water
Lighting up a ciggie in a no smoking carriage
Suggesting Mary Whitehouse had sex before marriage
Giving Brigitte Bardot a real mink stole
Telling Ray Charles that you can't stand soul
Breastfeeding babies in Oxford Street
Or remarking on Diana's enormous feet.

So if my sister's marriage goes wrong should I intervene?
I'd have to say no
I'd have to say no:
And is it wrong to say you don't like Torvill and Dean:
I have to say yes.
It's rather unwise.

Picking your nose at an interview
Keeping your mouth open when you chew
Hogging the loo when there's a queue
It's taboo it's taboo it's taboo

Doing a bunk on your wedding day
Sleeping with your brother when his wife's away
Admitting to the world you're a lousy lay
It's taboo it's taboo it's taboo.

Taboo is when you break Society's rule
Like having a pee in the swimming pool
Supporting the South African Tour of the Lions
Confessing that you can't bear Jeremy Irons
Going on a date with Maggie Thatcher's son
Standing in the tube with your flies undone
Then exposing yourself to a girl like me
Or declaring that you vote for the S.D.P.

So if you ask me if I can point in public and snigger:
I'd have to say no,
It's so terribly rude:
And is it wrong to tell a man you wish it was bigger?
I'd have to say yes:
They're such sensitive souls.

Discussing the details of your diarrhoea
Giving your best friend gonorrhoea
Sticking your tongue in the vicar's ear
It's taboo it's taboo it's taboo

Breaking wind as you meet the Queen
Telling her a joke that she finds obscene
Admitting to knowing Dillie Keane
It's taboo it's taboo it's taboo

So if you ask me if taboo is a crazy convention
I have to say yes
I have to say yes
And if you ask me if I've included all the other taboos
    that we've read about because we did an awful lot of research
    for this song, we read Fraser and Freud and Jung, and there
    were lots and lots of other taboos that we wanted to mention:
I have to say no
Why man?
Because they're taboo.

Words: Adèle Anderson, Marilyn Cutts, Dillie Keane
Music: Dillie Keane
© 1984

CHAPTER SIX

BIG IN BATTERSEA

or

'Fascinating Who?'

Our first two gigs for *Stop the Week* were successful enough, and we became regulars on the show, appearing one month in every three. But it wasn't our first broadcast. Just as we were about to go and pre-record 'Queen of Country', the sad song of a mega-seller denied a place in *Who's Who*, we were rung up by my pal Amanda Walker who works as a news editor on Capital Radio, and who'd been promoting our cause there since the days of Shades. Could we, she asked, do three songs live on the evening show that very night as the Sadista Sisters had had to cancel?

'Why waste all those nerves on just one gig?' said Marilyn, so we agreed to do it and thus were on the radio twice in the one weekend before doing even one live gig.

The *STW* commissions are a 48 hour nightmare.

Wednesday 4.30 pm	*I ring Michael Ember, the producer, to find out if he has a subject for us.*
	'Ah Dillie, my dear!' The immaculate middle-European voice purrs down the wire. 'What can I do for you?'
	'I just wondered if you might possibly have one of the topics for the programme.'
	'Ah no, I'm afraid not. I have discussed a few topics with Robert [Robinson] but ah, nothing concrete as yet. Why don't you phone me in the morning?'
Thursday 10.15 am	*Another phone call.*
	'Ah, good morning Dillie. Only one topic so far I'm afraid.'
	'Oh, don't worry — anything will do.'
	'Yes, well there has been quite a lot in the news this week about the announcement that British telephone boxes are to be painted yellow, so we thought we might take that as a starting point to discuss telephone boxes in general.'
	'Telephone boxes . . . ?'

FASCINATING A
Keane, Richardso
Cutts

BEST SHOW, by an Irish
that I've seen on the Fri
two weeks. This late-
cabaret at the Circuit, w
and sung by three very
professional actresses, is
minutes of laughter and del

To a battered ragtime pi
they do solos, trios and p
songs, plus some clowni
about and joking. The tunes
fine, it's the content of t
songs that's so wickedly funn
They satirise diet suburbi
housewifely blues, Communism
heavy choir singing, husbands,
visit to the doctor, separation,
punk music, the bomb and half-
a-dozen other angst-making subjects. The pace never flags, the
singing itself is good and the
laughs erupt about six to
the minute. Only exhaustion
stopped more encores.

George Duthie

'*Yes. How maddening they are, etcetera etcetera. How whenever you find one that works, you don't have the right money and so on . . . Everybody has something to say about them, don't you agree?*'

'*I see. Well, um, thanks. Could you phone me when you've got something else?*'

10.27 am	*Marilyn arrives, three minutes early.*
10.45 am	*Adèle arrives, fifteen minutes late. We discuss telephone boxes exhaustively, and their potential as the subject for a song. We draw a blank. Marilyn goes to buy fish for lunch — essential brain food.*
11.00 am	*Coffee break.*
11.15 am	*Lizzie used to arrive, forty-five minutes late, hair dripping wet and eating a kebab. 'I'm so SORRY! My aerobics class went overtime, and I had to have a shower, and then I was absolutely starving . . .'*
11.30 am	*Coffee break.*
11.40 am	*Phone rings. All rush to it. Rats! It's Rachel, our agent. We need topics, not idle chit-chat about future bookings!*
11.50 am	*Phone rings. Thank heaven, it's Michael.*

'*Ah, hello Dillie. How are you getting on with telephone boxes?*'

'*Um, fine. Fine.*' *Must disguise the lack of inspiration at all costs.*

'*Do you need another subject?*'

'*Oh, well, um, it's always good to have a choice . . .*'

'*True, true. Well, we have decided that the main theme of the programme will be Stately Homes.*'

Stately Homes? Our faces fall even further. Surely no-one can improve on Noel Coward's song, 'The Stately Homes of England'? I am attacked by a feeling of inadequacy. Marilyn is a tower of strength, and leaps off to the library over the road to do research. Adèle and I have another coffee break.

12.30 am	*Marilyn returns awash with quotations written on the backs of last week's song lyrics — we are busy saving trees. Meanwhile, I have had an idea. The address of an old friend has come to me . . . 'Number Four the Willows' . . . it has a musical ring to it . . . Perhaps we*

The first official snap. (Note Dillie is now a natural blonde.)

Inset: The first important review — George Duthie obviously saw us on a better night than Ian Albery. (The Scotsman, *8th September 1983*) *could write it from the point of view of someone opening their semi-d to the public? I try out half a verse:*

> *Number Four the Willows*
> *Is open to the public*
> *Ev'ry day from ten to half past four:'*

12.35 am   *Marilyn goes to the lavatory to concentrate — it's the only peaceful place in the flat.*

12.40 am   *Marilyn re-appears. She has completed the verse.*

> *'Notice as you enter*
> *Our pedimented architrave*
> *Framing rather blah-blah-blah our neo-Georgian door.'*

I suggest 'tastefully' for that missing word. We all agree it's a good start, and get down to work.

4.15 pm   *I am in the Slough of Despond. It's the worst song in the history of the world: we'll never get another job. Marilyn loses patience with me and sends me out to buy myself a Mars Bar.*

5.00 pm   *The Mars Bar lives up to every claim. Inspiration flows.*

7.00 pm   *The lyrics are more or less finished, and I have a vague idea for a tune. Marilyn goes home, and Adèle and I get drunk. (Only difference with Lizzie was that she simply needed two glasses of wine to get sloshed — Adèle is as expensive as I am.)*

9.30 pm   *Adèle staggers home. I go straight to bed, pooped.*

Friday   *I get up and write the music, usually in my head*
6.30 am   *because I don't want to wake my flatmates, and add the harmonies during breakfast.*

10.23 am   *Marilyn arrives, seven and a half minutes early, catching me still in my nightie. Her punctuality makes me paranoid. She takes the completed song to the photocopying shop: she has bagged this job and we suspect her of having a flirtation with 'The Beamish Boy' who does the photocopying.*

11.00 am   *Adèle/Lizzie arrives. We start learning the song.*

1.00 pm   *We race to Broadcasting House to pre-record it.*

4.30 pm   *The talking heads start arriving — we must be finished.*

Somehow, we always manage to do it in spite of the horrendously tight schedule, and some good songs have come out of it: the subjects are usually so bizarre that they force us to write songs that are equally singular.

Once we were presented with what seemed to be an impossible commission. Marilyn rang Michael on the Wednesday evening, and for a change he had already hit on one theme for the panel to talk about.

'Ah Marilyn, nice to speak to you. Yes, we already have a topic for this week. It's "My Favourite Tool".'

'Pardon, Michael?' said Marilyn, not quite believing her ears.

'My Favourite Tool.'

Still uncertain, Marilyn asked, 'Sorry, how do you spell that last word?'

'T-O-O-L: tool. You know, spirit level, hammer. Everybody has a favourite chisel in their tool box. You must have had a tape-measure or something you were particularly fond of at school.'

'Um, not really, but thanks anyhow. I'll ring again in the morning.'

We didn't know what to make of it. Spirit levels? Tape-measures? We were very depressed, and agreed not to even try to get any writing done that night, but to wait till we heard what the other topic was.

Marilyn arrived the next morning, her face shining. 'I've had an idea!'

'So've I,' I said defensively.

'All right, you say your idea first and then I'll say mine and we'll see whose is best.'

'No, you say yours first.'

'Well, I've written a rough couplet which sort of gives the basic idea,' said Marilyn. A couplet? She was already one step ahead of me.

'It's not very good, but it could be a start . . .
  "There's nothing that a woman can't put right
  With a hairpin, a nail-file and a pair of tights."'

'How extraordinary!' I exclaimed. 'That's almost exactly the same as my idea! I thought we could write a song about a pair of tights and how useful they are in any emergency, like . . .'

'Like mending a broken fan-belt!'

'Yes, quite!' I said. 'Or plugging a leaking dyke like the man who saved Holland by sticking his finger in the hole . . .'

'And what about foiling a bank robbery?' suggested Marilyn brilliantly.

Just to be sure we weren't going to be given an even *better* topic, Marilyn rang Michael.

'Hello Michael, it's Marilyn again. I was just wondering if you had that other subject for us?'

'Ah, Marilyn, yes I have. It's cock-ups.'

We stuck with 'My Favourite Tool' and it's still in our repertoire.

MY FAVOURITE TOOL*

Well I was walking down the road about a month ago
I saw this broken down car and I thought, 'Hello:
I think I'll go and take a look.'
Well this chap was poring over his maintenance book.
He had hot drop forged molybdenum steel blades:
Spanners and ratchets of various grades:
He had a fuel injection pipe nut wrench,
All laid out on a metal frame bench . . .
Well I looked at his motor and I said, real cool,
'What you need, mush, is the proper tool:
Yer fan belt's bust, put on yer warnin' lights
And I'll fix it now with a pair of tights.'
He said 'A pair of tights?'
I said 'Right:
Tights.'

   Seam-free, micromesh or surgical support:
   They'll fit you if you're tall and they'll fit you if you're short.

Well I was walkin' past the bank when I heard the alarm;
A robb'ry was in progress but I wasn't unarmed
Having just bought a six-pair economy pack,
So I burst through the door and said, 'Please stand back!'
I filled a pair with soot from the bucket by the door,
Slugged a villain with the foot, he went sprawlin' on the floor:
Then combining a slip knot with a drop lasso,
I tripped up robber Number Two.
Well you could tell the rest was thick 'cos they 'ad stockin's on
   their 'eads
So I tied the ends together, sayin' 'Gimme the bread.'
Then I gagged 'em and bound 'em with the last pair of the day:
I used ladder resistant so they wouldn't run away.
Hooray
For tights.

*Words and music by Dillie Keane: © 1984 EMI Music Publishing Ltd. London WC2H 0LD

There's rose toe, sandal foot, ribbed or without,
Reinforced gusset or sheer throughout:

Last year, on a trip to the Netherlands,
I was cruisin' around with my friend called Hans,
When Hans cried 'Look! Emergency!
There's a crack in the dyke around the Zuyder Zee!'
I saw that the trickle would soon become a flood
And so, to mix a metaphor, I nipped it in the bud,
Hans ran to call the burghers while I hitched up me clothes 'n'
Wriggled out of me Strumpfelhosen:
I screwed 'em up in a nice tight ball,
And I rammed 'em into that crack in the wall:
When the rescuers saw that I'd held back the sea,
They decided to name a tulip after me,
Called
'Tights'.

There's no better tool for setting things to rights,
And that's why Superman always wears –
Tights.

Above: Lizzie demonstrating the length of the fissure in the dyke.

Marilyn and Lizzie were now out of work with no definite job offers, and selfishly I was delighted because it meant that we could concentrate on getting some live gigs. Marilyn found out about a new venue called Jongleurs that was opening in Battersea so we auditioned and were soon appearing there regularly.

Encouraged I rang up the organisers of all the venues listed in *Time Out* and our list of bookings grew longer. I persuaded a bloke called Lawrence to book us at the Hemingford Arms, even though he'd never heard of us, and we arrived at the prearranged time to do our sound check.

We went up to the cabaret room and found a young man of about 24 standing by the sound desk: he had a blonde-tipped, spiky top hairdo and appeared to be humping the table as he thrust his hips rhythmically towards it in time to the unbearably loud music.

'Excuse me!' I shouted. 'I'm looking for Lawrence!!!'

No luck. His eyes were closed, his jaw sagged as he grooved, and his hips continued to thrust.

'I'M LOOKING FOR SOMEONE CALLED LAWRENCE!'

He registered. ''S me,' he said.

'WE'RE FASCINATING AIDA.' He nodded, funking away. 'WE'VE COME TO DO OUR SOUND CHECK.'

''S cool, man.' He waved us over to the stage area, but it was impossible to do a sound check with the music blaring. Unwillingly, Lawrence turned it down a point. We protested again. Eventually, he turned it off looking put out, and we got on with the sound check. I tried the piano. It hadn't been tuned since Chopin died and wobbled precariously on the edge of the rickety podium, so we leaned it against the wall at a drunken angle. It seemed safer and couldn't make it sound any worse.

Next we examined the changing room. This consisted of a tiny screen in the corner behind which all three of us had to change. We discovered we could just manage to change one at a time if the other two sat on the table.

'Where are we supposed to do our make-up?' wailed Lizzie, fumbling around in the gloom.

''S a mirror in the toilet,' said Lawrence, still getting down.

Before the show, Lawrence called us to His Imperial Presence.

'Fascinating Ader? Yeah. I'm puttin' you on last 'cos you make the most noise, okay? Now you gotta know the rules. Artistes are not allowed to go through the audience durin' the show. Right? Artistes are not allowed to sit in the chairs to watch the show: they may only stand at the back. Okay? Artistes appearin' in the second half must go behind the screen durin' the interval. Right? Artistes are not allowed to get friends in free. Okay? These are my rules, and

I don't break 'em for anybody. Okay? Okay. Right.'

Then he sloped off to do a bit more hanging out. At the end of the show he ran up to us a changed man.

'Excuse me, Fascinating Aïda? That was a *really* great . . . I mean, the audience *really* . . . er . . . would you be willing to do . . . um . . . would next Friday be at all possible? Please?'

The flak over our name was unbelievable. My entire family and all my friends rang one by one to tell me what an appalling and pretentious name Fascinating Aïda was, and besides, telephonists could never get it right.

I'd ring some radio producer who'd expressed an interest in hiring us. 'Hello,' I'd say to the receptionist, 'I'd like to speak to so-and-so.'

'What name is it please?'

'It's Dillie Keane of Fascinating Aïda.'

'Billie Green of Fascinating Who?'

'No, **D**illie **K**eane of Fascinating **AI-EEE-DA**.'

''Hankyooooo . . . Mr. So-and-so, it's Tillie Deans of Fascinating Ida.'

We were about to give in to the pressure and re-name ourselves The Doxies when Maria Kempinska, who runs Jongleurs, called me.

'Dillie, I hear you want to change your name: is this true?'

I told her it was.

'Well, for a start you can't because all the publicity for next week has been printed, and besides, it's a *wonderful* name. So don't be daft.'

Thank you, Maria.

I don't remember much detail about the first six months except that I was constantly panicking. Live bookings mounted up. Panic – would Lizzie lose her way? Radio commissions increased. Panic – would we ever write another song? We did our first telly show for HTV in August. Panic – would my double chin kill my career in television? Lawrence asked us to do a gig at The Rock Garden in Covent Garden. Panic – there was no piano. My friend Amanda Walker lent me £500 to buy an electric piano. Panic – would I ever be able to pay her back?

Somehow we muddled through, and at the beginning of September 1983 we went to the Edinburgh Festival for the first time. Matthew Bannister, Amanda's young man, had asked us to be in a revue he was putting on in the final week of the Festival. Two days before we were due to depart for Scotland, Maria Kempinska rang us up. A sudden cancellation had made a last-minute vacancy in another venue and at a later time than our revue – would we be willing to take it even though we had no advance publicity? We accepted.

Adèle and Dillie demonstrate the versat[il]ity of tights.

Annihilate your rival: send your enemie[s] packing with a tights-catapult and an appropriate missile (in this case, a can o[f] hair spray). Fashion note: spots worn on [the] body detract from those on the face.

Use your old hose to fashion gloriously [c]razy headwear: a Covent Garden artist poses with Adèle (sporting a medieval-style bonnet) and Dillie (wearing an ever-pop[ular] turban). Both hats are made from tights incredible but true! A passing felon mod[els] the latest in bank robbing gear.

Bring more booze home: when Adèle ha[s] completely filled her pannier with wines [of] the great chateaux, she slings a couple m[ore] round her neck, onion-seller style, down [the] legs of her pantie-hose.

Bored with your job? Adèle discovers th[at] laddered tights tied together make an effective rope ladder.

We arrived in Edinburgh to discover that the venue was a tent in a hole in the ground. It had been raining steadily for weeks and the place was a sea of mud. Our show began at twenty to one in the morning, and we only got the booking because the cast of the previous show, *The Rock Tartuffe* (Lawrence's first foray into production), had had such an appalling time that they fled after sobbing in the portacabin toilets for a week.

That week was crazy. We'd spend all day from 10.30 distributing leaflets in the rain, and at 7.00 perform the revue at the Herriot Watt Theatre. Then we'd dash off to some club or other to do a twenty minute 'taster' to try and entice people into either of our shows. At midnight, we'd wade through the mire to our nissen hut to change, wade back through the bog to our tent in wellies and stage frocks, clutching our high heels, and at 12.40 do the FA show. At about 3.00 am, we'd crawl into bed, knackered.

For the first three days our audience consisted almost entirely of Matthew and the others from the revue which was very loyal of them but a bit disheartening for us seeing the same six faces in the audience night after night. And however much they loved the songs, they couldn't keep laughing with the same gusto at the same jokes every single time.

On the Thursday, we got a wonderful review in *The Scotsman*, and the punters started to pour in with and in spite of the rain. Our spirits soared. On the Friday, Ian Albery of the famous theatrical family (the Carringtons of the West End) came to the show, and afterwards came backstage and politely savaged us.

'It would be a waste of my time and yours,' he said, in a quiet but devastating way, 'if I were to flatter you. You have some quite good material, but it needs a lot of work. You have no real identity, and clearly don't think about your material nearly enough. Your appearance is second rate – you must get some kind of a coherent look. The patter between the songs is dreadful. You could go on playing at Festivals for the rest of your lives, I expect, but is that what you want? You'll never get anywhere the way you are at the moment. If you're really serious about this, get a director now.'

Thoroughly dejected, I went off to join some friends at an all night Italian restaurant in the Caledonian Road. As I got out of the taxi in the driving rain, a small dark figure huddled under an umbrella on the pavement rushed forward to claim the cab.

It was Nica.

There was an embarrassing moment as we changed places: we had barely spoken in two years. It took me two seconds to make up my mind.

'Nica: we need a director.'

It took her about the same length of time. 'Okay,' she said, challengingly, and disappeared into the night.

Our last gig with Lizzie was a ten day run in the Dublin Theatre Festival in October. We arrived there the night before our first performance, and as soon as we landed I went down to the Project Arts Theatre to check it out: we were appearing late night after another play and I felt I ought to have a look at their set to see how we'd have to adapt. Brian Power, the stage manager, met me and took me into the auditorium.

I nearly fainted. What I remembered as an ordinary box-like room with seating on two sides had been transformed to represent the aftermath of a nuclear holocaust. The nose of a wrecked aeroplane rose from the centre of the floor; great heaps of garbage lay strewn all around connected by planks: the mangled corpse of a defunct aviator lay ghoulishly face down in the rubbish, and strange things hung from the ceiling, increasing the atmosphere of chaos. Odd banks of seats encircled the room, facing every which way.

'What in God's name is this?' I gasped.

'It's the set for the Polish play,' said Brian proudly: he'd designed the damn thing.

'And where are we supposed to (a) stand and (b) put the piano?' I asked, gathering my wits.

'Em, well, ye could put the piano over there,' said Brian, indicating the only flat area three feet long and two feet wide and stuck in between two small stands with chairs on them, 'and the other two girls could stand over there.' Brian pointed airily to another tiny space nestling between the piles of debris at the far end of the room.

'And where do you propose that the audience should sit?'

Brian waved his arms vaguely: 'In the seats, sure. I mean, it's not ideal, but you'll have to make do with it, Dill.'

'Well, let me tell you,' I said in my steeliest manner, 'that I have no intention of performing an intimate, sophisticated cabaret satirising suburban angst and the foibles of the middle-classes in the middle of the Polish vision of a nuclear winter. Nor will I do a show when 70% of the audience will be looking at the backs of our dresses for the entire evening'.

'Ah now, I wouldn't worry about the audience. You'll be lucky to get thirty people a night. The Festival Club's next door,' said Brian, still insensible to the degree of fury raging in my bosom. 'It's you or a late night drinking licence, Dill. And I know which I'd choose. Now d'ye fancy a pint?'

I saw red. 'Now just look here,' I said, jabbing my finger into Brian's chest. 'I want a stage, big enough for all three of us *with* the piano, at one end of the room so that the *whole* audience can see us *all* clearly *all* the time. I will come in tomorrow morning, and if you *haven't* got something acceptable organised, we will catch the first boat home. And when hundreds of eager punters arrive and find there's no show, *you* can bloody well explain why we're not here.' And I marched out of the theatre, seething.

The next day I came in and found Lizzie and Marilyn sitting ashen faced in the large white foyer that doubled as an art gallery.

'Dillie, have you *seen* the theatre?' they cried.

'Yes, and I can assure you that under no circumstances . . . hang on a minute . . .' I looked around me, and ran off to find Brian.

'Brian!' I shouted. 'We'll do the show right here in the barn!'

After a lot of arguing about fire regulations and lighting, they finally realised that I was not only implacable, I was right, and we did the show in the foyer. And I still get a glow of satisfaction when I think of the packed, cheering audiences and the large number of people turned away with the sign 'Full House'.

It's just as well I didn't go to Poland.

Lizzie left us the day after we finished in Dublin. She'd been offered a job she couldn't refuse and went back to Canada to do a major play in Toronto. We were very sad, but Lizzie had always been very straightforward about her attitude to Fascinating Aïda – she loved it, but it would always come second to her acting career.

Lizzie's departure forced Marilyn and I into making a big decision as to whether Fascinating Aïda was a career or a hobby. Up till that moment, it had been an occasionally hilarious diversion that had given us the chance to develop different skills and to keep performing when we would have otherwise been idle: a long period of unemployment can dull ability and damage confidence irreparably.

As far as I was concerned, there was no choice. I'm not easy to cast for one thing, and I could see a future chocabloc with yawning voids of unemployment. Being obsessively perfectionist, I'm frequently crabbit and difficult to work with, and I loved being with Marilyn who, though more self-controlled than me, was every bit as technically demanding. For the first time in my life, I was working with someone who was on my wavelength: we collaborated well and had already written a few of our best songs – 'The Herpes Tango' and 'Kay Why?' being the two most notable. Our alter egos, the Brontë Sisters (more of whom later), had started to assert themselves in the show and were a great hit with the audiences. We were getting regular bookings and had done our first television show, a comedy programme for HTV that featured Screaming Lord Sutch amongst others. Offers were rolling in thick and fast for work that would take us at least through till January, and Marilyn's then agent, Michelle Braidman, was happy to act for us till we could find the right variety agency. Above all, we were writing and performing our own material and we were our own bosses, so to abandon FA now seemed like utter folly.

Marilyn wasn't quite so blindingly certain as I was. Where I found an acting career frustrating and often humiliating, Marilyn loved it: she's easier to cast, for one thing, and had rarely been out of work since she'd left drama school. And though she revelled in the writing side of FA's work, becoming a cabaret artiste had never been a part of her master plan. With hindsight, I now realise that she probably could have dropped the whole project without much regret when Lizzie left, but she's a quiet soul and not one for shouting her feelings from the rooftop, as I am. Armoured as I was in my enormous enthusiasm, I didn't discern that early lack of ease in Marilyn: it was not unhappiness then, but a vague sense of discomfort which later became great unhappiness.

To be fair to myself, I don't think I was riding roughshod over her feelings. She could see for herself that we had done extraordinarily well in the six months we'd been in operation: we were earning just about enough to live on and our success at the Dublin Theatre Festival was more than encouraging because it was the first time we'd ever done our own proper show on our own terms, and we had been one of the biggest hits of the festival. This was before Nica had had a chance to start working properly with us, and Marilyn was extremely excited by the fact that Nica was to join the team.

So we had a long talk, and decided that we'd put too much work into it to abandon it now. We'd give it a total of two years from our starting date, and if in that time we hadn't made significant progress, we'd chuck it in with no hard feelings. We planned for the day when we'd be able to do FA for six months of the year and our own thing for the remainder of the time, and neither of us had the slightest notion that we'd probably be in our fifties before we got that far.

We put an advert in *The Stage* and held auditions. About thirty girls applied, and there was one who was outstanding. Her name was Glenda Smith.

SEW ON A SEQUIN

F Dillie Keane 1984

When life has got you down;
You're broke, you're on your uppers;
And you don't know who to call your friend;
When for weeks and months you've roughed it
And your pekingese has snuffed it;
And you feel you've really reached the bitter end;
When your mother-in-law has gone
To Gretna Green with your son
And the river, yes, the river's your only hope:
Don't do it, no, don't jump!
Take a tip from me, you chump;
And listen, for here's the only way to cope . . .

Sew on a sequin, it's sure to cheer you up;
Sew on a sequin when you've drained life's bitter cup.
Sequins will brighten up the oldest shabby dress;
Sequins are guaranteed to bring you happiness.
A sequin is such a little thing;
But sure as hell, you know that it'll bring
You through when you've got writer's block;
Yes it's easier to smile
As you face each fearful trial
When you've got a bit of heaven on your frock.

You think you've reached rock bottom —
Those low down blues, you gottem;
'Cause your fiance's made some other girl his wife;
You're at the altar, jilted,
The flowers are all wilted;
You're tumbling through the waste disposal chute of life;
Keep your chin up, don't be a funk;
Pack your trousseau in a trunk;
You've no money? well, go out and sell the ring;
Paint some lipstick and powder on please,
And throw away those dungarees;
And go and make some other man your king . . .

Tack on some tinsel, you owe it to yourself;
Add some diamante and you'll climb back off the shelf;
Fix on some feathers, ruche some tulle around your hem;
Then you can face the future with the right amount of phlegm.
Ladies, we always must a—
—ttempt to keep our lustre;
And you never know the passion you'll arouse;
So darlings, don't be bitter,
Be lib'ral with the glitter;
And embroider lots of moonbeams on your blouse.

Sew on a sequin when you've felt fate's piercing dart;
If you're in the equinox of life, 'twill cheer your heart;
Gather your organza, shimmer shine be gay;
Don't give in to tears; just emulate the Milky Way.
Though a sequin's wee, it twinkles;
Takes the focus off your wrinkles;
A sequin more is e'er a trouble less;
So ply your needle through that hole,
Or just glue one to your mole,
And strew a spot of stardust;
Ev'ry girl from near and far must
Strew a spot of stardust on your dress.

Words and Music: Dillie Keane © 1984

CHAPTER SEVEN

CHANGES

It clearly wasn't going to be easy to replace Lizzie who not only had a gorgeous voice but was also funny and beautiful. Nor could we bank on the fact that anyone would be willing to take the risk of throwing in their lot with an extremely unorthodox, unheard-of group for an irregular salary. But when Glenda arrived off the train for her audition having come from a Butlins Holiday Camp where she was spending the summer as a redcoat, we took to her immediately. Up to this moment, we hadn't seen anyone who'd taken our fancy, but Glenda's letter on pink paper had made us laugh a lot: besides which, she had impressive credentials having studied opera at the Royal Scottish Academy of Music and Drama.

She was a tall, curvaceous girl with glossy dark brown hair, almond eyes, an olive complexion and a heavenly voice. At this time Marilyn alternated singing the middle harmony with Lizzie, so it seemed logical to look for someone with the same range who could take turns to sing the top line. Glenda's voice wasn't one of those opera voices which are all warble and no charm: it floated, still and pure, with a surprising strength, and was a joy to work with.

Better still, she was a charm to be with: ready for anything and phased by nothing. After telling her about ourselves, and singing her some of our songs, she said she'd love to be in Fascinating Aïda, and so it was decided that she should join us right away.

As soon as she'd learned the songs, which took her just a few days, we went into the craziest work schedule we've ever known. We were still doing songs regularly for *Stop the Week* when we took on a series of six songs for Saturday TVAM, and another half dozen for a late Monday night show on Thames called *After Hours*. We were always on when anyone with any sense was tucked up and in the Land of Nod, which meant that we could learn the mysterious ways of telly without too many people realising what greenhorns we were. On top of that, we were doing at least three gigs a week in and around London. As each song took at least a day to write and another to rehearse and learn, we were working flat out.

Then at Christmas we did our one and only panto. In spite of appearing regularly on television, we were only ever paid the lowest possible fee, and Marilyn and I were in hock up to our elbows as our earnings for the first six months had been risible. The Christmas present list loomed: a vision of eight disappointed small boys (my nephews) rose before my eyes: my mind was made up. So for all my loathing of pantomime, I found myself at the Battersea Arts Centre

for six weeks in *Aladdin — A Zany Pantomime!* featuring
Fascinating Aïda as the pit musicians and song writers.

We'd been under the impression that we'd be handed a script
some time before rehearsals began, and that we'd arrive on the day
of the first read-through with a neat pile of lead sheets to the songs.
No such luck: it turned out to be one of those make-it-up-as-you-go-
along jobs that I love so well.

A week of devising went by before we got so much as a rough
script, and all we did was sit in rehearsals, wondering when our
promised acting roles would materialise and waiting for instructions
while the rest of the cast improvised happily. Eventually they started
deciding where they wanted the songs — twelve of them, to be
written, set to music and learned in two weeks. We were called for
rehearsals all day, then had to write the songs at night, bring them in
fully harmonised and teach them to the cast the next day. This was
disastrous for us, as we'd set aside those evenings to write the music
for a documentary about health farms. A director called Mark
Chapman who Lizzie knew had asked us to provide the incidental
music for a film he was making for the *40 Minutes* series on BBC 2.
We were delighted, but when the panto started eating into the time
we'd set aside to get the music done, we got desperate.

Phone messages from Mark would be waiting when I got home:
could he *please* have one slow and one fast version of 'The Jogging
Song', an entirely new song about cellulite and 18.2 seconds on tape
of the opening piano music by tomorrow morning. It took me four
hours to work out how to get 18.2 seconds worth of tune to sound
coherent, let alone fulfil his other requests. And this was on top of
having to write new songs for Widow Twanky et al, complete with
harmonies for us and the rest of the cast.

I was getting a maximum of three hours sleep a night, working till
2.30 and getting up at 5.30 just to try and keep the tide of work from
engulfing me completely. And most of the onus was on me as I
found collaborating far too slow when we didn't have the luxury of a
whole day to write a song. I lived on pot noodles, Mars Bars and
gallons of white wine. Lack of sleep began to tell on me. I started to
hallucinate: I didn't know what day it was and I was completely
paranoid. Marilyn would tell me something, I'd forget it and then
accuse her of trying to make me go mad when she reminded me. I
was not well at all.

Panto opened, and the work continued unabated as we had yet
more telly commitments. On Christmas Day we appeared on TVAM
— we had been commissioned to write a seasonal song to be sung in
the early hours of Christmas morning. The brief was: no satire, no
scepticism, and certainly no cynicism, just a 'nice' song for the

F.A. in Incarnation No. 2 with the lovely Glenda Smith. This was a shot taken for an F.A. Christmas card, hence the festive atmosphere.

Yuletide Morn. I found this a particularly difficult commission as I regard the festive season as being roughly on a par with a plague of boils.

However, I ignored my feelings and set to work on a suitably syrupy song. And syrupy it was. It was like drowning in a vat of treacle. I can honestly say it was the ghastliest song ever to defile the airwaves since 'I, I Who Have Nothing'.

Worse still, we were to be attired in grisly Xmas frockettes. Wardrobe had hired three completely nefandous red velvet micro-minis with fake fur trim and dinky wee hoods, and bows for our hair. We looked like Baby Jane multiplied by three.

I arrived at TVAM at the appointed time with what felt like a pair of golf balls in my neck where my lymph nodes ought to be. Shivering with the ague, and with terrible swollen glands, I performed the song like Boris Karloff as the monster.

Somehow, I got through the rehearsals, performance and jolly fun at the end of the programme. I dimly recall hordes of appalling tots screaming their heads off. I just wanted to kick their heads off and only my enfeebled state stopped me. Eventually I sloped off to my empty flat where I slept for three days until I was rescued by my sister who took me to her home to recuperate. I was quite ill for ten days, and as soon as I was up, it was straight back into the maelstrom.

Dillie working hard with a difficult audience

After panto finished, Glenda decided that Fascinating Aïda wasn't for her. Again, we were sad, but we felt she had made the right decision, if only for the reason that she wanted to sing pop music. She agreed to go on working with us until the end of March, so that we had time to find someone new.

Finding a new person for a group is like looking for a husband or wife. You start out with a clear idea of what you want, and end up with something completely different. You reject a large number of people who, on the face of it, have everything you need, in favour of the one you've taken a fancy to. When we chose Glenda, she was far and away the best candidate, and yet a few months later we were back to square one.

One of the biggest problems of a group is achieving a balance between the personalities. Everyone needs to feel they have their place in the group. When Lizzie, Marilyn and I started out, we were all on an equal footing. When Glenda joined, the balance changed. Either Marilyn and I didn't let Glenda find her place, or she wasn't interested in the management side of the job – I'm not sure which. The truth is probably somewhere in between the two. Glenda certainly made a significant musical contribution to the group and was by no means a sleeping partner: but being a member of Fascinating Aïda is in some ways a life sentence, and so it wasn't surprising when she opted out.

LIEDER

Doesn't matter if you sing out of tune
So long as you're German.
Doesn't matter if you can hardly croon
So long as you're German.
So if you haven't got a note in your head,
Put on a silly accent instead,
And people will stop wishing you were dead,
So long as you're German.

Doesn't matter if the notes are all wrong,
And people are squirmin'.
Just make the tune up as you go along,
Pretend you're German.
And if your voice sounds like it's coming through a strainer,
Sing it out of synch, like Marlene,
And soon you'll be compared to Lotte Lenya,
Who *was* German.

Nich hin auf slenen sprecht gesang Zauberflote wunderbar
Johnny
Wiener schnitzel, Boris Becker, sturm und drang, Cooch Behar
Johnny.

So if you've ever wondered what you have to do
To sound like a Hun.
Just chain smoke from the tender age of two,
That's how it's done.
And when the audiences are all walking out,
Just make believe that you're a Kraut,
Then open your mouth and shout
In German,
In German,
In Deutsche,
Jahwohl.

Words: Adèle Anderson, Marilyn Cutts and Dillie Keane
Music: Dillie Keane
© 1985

JAZZ FEVER

More from Adèle . . .

It took me ten years to figure out how to get my Equity card, but once I did it was a relatively simple matter. In 1972 when I left university, the only way to get one was by landing a job with a theatre company, usually as an Acting ASM (Assistant Stage Manager). These jobs were limited and mostly they were snapped up each season by a lucky few from the hordes of eager hopefuls pouring out of the drama schools and university drama departments, ready to give their all after three years training. It helped tremendously if you were the child of a famous actor or the friend of a director. I was neither and so got trampled in the rush.

Later, when Equity incorporated the Variety Artists' Federation they encouraged their members to apply for Equity cards. Now, if you could juggle, eat fire or ride an elephant, the union welcomed you. I could do none of these, nor could I play the piano (see page 11). I toyed with the idea of becoming a stripper (a friend told me someone she knew had obtained a card this way) but I once worked in a strip club as a disc jockey (that's another story) so I knew what the girls had to put up with and it wasn't for me. Besides which, most of the jobs were in Bahrain or Kuala Lumpur and I loathe hot climates. One day, as I soaped myself in the shower, my flatmate hammered on the door and told me to keep the noise down as he was trying to get romantic with a new love and my rendition of 'Don't Go Breaking My Heart' was putting him off. 'That's it!' I thought. 'I'll take up singing again.'

I placed an ad in Melody Maker.

'Female vocalist, amazing vocal range, seeks musicians for jazz gigs.'

I had a few replies and followed up all of them. Most people looked at me askance as soon as I opened my mouth. If we were going to work together it was obvious they'd have to transpose everything. The ad appeared three weeks running but it wasn't until a fortnight after the last entry that I struck lucky. A man called Glenn telephoned and asked if I was still looking for musicians. He was not a musician himself, he said, but he knew where to find some. He did, too, and though they were by no means enamoured of my singing he cajoled them into working with me.

Pretty soon we were working well together. I began by recording backing vocals for a collection of musicians called Hot Summer Night *but it was live work I needed and so* Cocktails With Adèle *was*

formed. *I'd certainly got better at choosing names since the days of Amajam.*

Mostly we performed around the East End of London, although we did have one heady night at Stringfellows, playing to an audience of six people, five of whom were staff. We had a residency at a pub in Bethnal Green.

To begin with we had good audiences. Naturally — all our friends came to see us. After a month or two they'd given all the support they could bear. Still, the owners didn't seem to mind the lack of clientèle. They even asked us to perform at their restaurant which was a barge moored on a canal. I didn't enjoy it much. We had to keep playing until the owners said we could stop. If they were having a party that meant we could be there for hours and there was no way off the boat except past them and their extremely large friends.

After a month of this, Ray, our pianist, decided he'd had enough and left. We were devastated. We changed our name to Jazz on the Rocks, which aptly summed up our situation, and worked with a succession of pianists but it was never the same. Then Clive, our drummer, decided to sell his drumkit and get married, but by then it didn't matter because we were out of a job. The pub owners had gone down for fifteen years. I'd often wondered where they got their money. Now I knew; from the bank, but unfortunately they acquired it outside normal banking hours.

I worked for a while with the Simon Purcell Trio but Simon did not care for the way I rewrote the lyrics of old standards. He wasn't all that keen on vocalists per se, feeling that they got in the way of the music, and so we parted amicably. I'm sorry to say that my parting with Glenn was not quite so amicable. He wanted me to carry on but I felt that that phase of my life was over. Still, I shall always be grateful to him. By the time we split I'd got my Equity card as I had the required amount of contracts, and I'd found my voice too. But no singing work.

When I first came to London I moved in with a friend on a temporary basis. It was ten years before I moved out. My friend was long gone by this time having given up hope of seeing the back of me (bear this in mind if you ever invite me for a visit) and he was succeeded by a series of flatmates. All the time I was there, a tall, handsome young man called John lived in the flat upstairs. He and I had seen each other through numerous crises but it wasn't until we both found ourselves living alone, having vowed there would be No More Flatmates for either of us, that we became really close friends. We could wake each other up at 2.00 am, that's how close we were. John always believed in me, both on a personal and professional level. He worked for a national newspaper but he was also a frustrated performer. I must admit I wasn't very supportive of his artistic aspirations, but his dreams of performing suddenly came true. I returned home from a short holiday to discover that he had entered a male striptease competition and won. No one was more flabbergasted than he was, particularly when told afterwards he should turn professional. The act, which he'd put together in one hour, was comedy and based on Italian quick change, with a surprising but effective climax. John asked me to become his manager, though that's too grand a title for what I did.

First we took his backing tape and edited it: then we choreographed every move. Finally, I chose his name — Johnny Fever (I was getting good at names by this time). We spent over a year travelling up and down the country. He concentrated on giving his all to hundreds of screaming women while I dealt with the business side — collecting his fee (my favourite bit), getting his contracts signed, and keeping him fed and watered.

It's amazing the difference it makes if an artist shows up with his manager. The owner of the venue treats him with respect, and for a stripper that's important. Though John billed himself as a comedy striptease artist, to bookers he was just another body they thought they could push around. Not when I was there.

I had another rôle to play. Sometimes he'd get pestered after the show by women wondering if he was as good offstage as he was on — know what I mean? On those occasions John would put his arm around me and say, 'Have you met my wife?' Oh yes, we had fun, and it was a welcome relief from the tedium of going to work each day. I might still be Mrs Johnny Fever if John himself hadn't unwittingly made it impossible for me to carry on. One night, he did something which led directly to my joining Fascinating Aïda.

A DAME THEY CALL DANGEROUS!

or
Enter Miss Anderson

A Steamy Novella

It was night.

Johnny Fever walked quickly through the streets of Soho. He ignored the call girls leering out of doorways, enticing him to the steamy basement rooms. He passed the pimps and the card sharps, and barely noticed the sex-shops with their discreet shop fronts. He was a man in a hurry.

Light rain began to fall, and the lamplights reflecting on the wet pavements gave an eerie glow to the night streets. Fever turned up the collar of his raincoat, and pulled his Homburg down over his face. Somewhere a saxophone wailed a mournful melody, but Fever didn't hear it. He paused briefly in a doorway to light a cigarette: then slipped away like a shadow through the crowd, up Shaftesbury Avenue and down into Seven Dials.

A few streets away, a policeman paused momentarily outside the innocent looking façade of the Donmar Warehouse Theatre, then moved on. There was no sign of the speakeasy going on inside, almost under the nose of Bow Street Police Station. The policeman read the innocuous theatre posters on the wall outside, then continued on his beat around Covent Garden. Fever watched him from a darkened alley way as he plodded down the street. Then like a flash he was at the door of the Donmar. He knocked with a quiet urgency.

After a few seconds, the door opened a crack.

'Whaddya want?' snarled a disembodied voice from within.

'I'm here to see Bertice Reading. Name of Johnny Fever.'

'Fever, huh? Can ya prove it?'

Johnny Fever produced a card from his pocket and handed it through the door. It was snatched from his hand.

'Sorry, not enough,' came the voice again. 'What's tonight's password?'

Fever thought for a moment. 'Nica Burns,' he hissed, acting on a hunch.

He'd done his research well. The door opened and he was hustled inside.

'Thanks,' he said, tossing a greenback to the 6'6'' doorman. 'What's your name?'

'Toby,' said the big lug.

'Okay Toby,' said Fever, fingering a roll of five pound notes. 'There's more where that came from if you can identify Nica Burns for me.'

Toby feasted his eyes on the roll of rhino in Fever's deceptively slim hand. 'Corn in Egypt, man . . .' he murmured. 'She's da little dame in da black dress. Top o' da stairs, coily black hair, kinda Spanish lookin'. Ya can't miss her.'

Fever pressed a couple of fivers into Toby's hand, and went up the stairs, pausing to check his hat and coat.

'That'll be twenty pence,' whined the hat check girl in a nasal voice. As Fever handed her his outer garments, she stared in open-mouthed admiration. He wore a torn, sleeveless, wet-look T-Shirt, which stretched across his bulging torso and showed off his muscular arms. Skin-tight black leather trousers caressed his lean, hard physique, and white leather boots completed the picture. Only Fever could dress like that and get away with it.

'Hey, are you Johnny Fever?' breathed the girl huskily.

'Yeah,' said Fever, nonchalantly. 'Who are you?'

'Candy,' she whispered, pouting her lips at him, 'and I'm free in an hour.'

'Thanks Candy,' said Fever. 'Be a good girl and hang on to this for me. And — don't mention it to anyone, okay?' He gave her the full Fever smile. She melted.

and took the gun he was handing her under cover of the coat. Women would do anything for Fever.

'Okay Johnny,' she said. 'Anything for you.'

'See you later.'

Johnny disappeared into the speakeasy. The place was packed with drunks and bootleggers, bright young things and not-so bright, not-so-young things. He leaned against the bar, and ordered himself a large bourbon. He drank it in one gulp, and looking through the thronging demi-monde, he suddenly saw the sculptured profile of the woman he loved. Oh, not loved in that way — she was too far above him to debase her with thoughts of carnal lust. To him, she was an alabaster goddess. She'd saved him, hadn't she?

He ordered another whisky and cast his mind back to the first time they'd met. He'd been a real Johnny No-Name then, a no-good, no-hope dancer in a deadbeat revue, working when he could as a gigolo and doing small-time kneecap jobs. He was on the skids, all right.

He'd come off the stage that particular night, covered in sweat, and walked into his dressing room. He didn't notice her as she was sitting in the chair behind the door.

'Good evening,' she said in that low, throaty voice he came to love so much. He wheeled round, startled.

'Who are you?' he snapped, his hand surreptitiously going for the gun he kept in his make-up box.

'I shouldn't bother,' said the lady coolly. 'I've taken the precaution of removing your gun, your stiletto and your cosh. So don't try any monkey business.'

'Whaddya want?' he snarled, suspiciously.

The lady took a couple of moments to think this one over. 'Let's just say,' she said carefully, 'that I want you.'

Fever smiled to himself as he remembered that. He'd been startled, non-plussed.

'Whaddya want me for? And who are ya anyhow?'

'My name's Adèle Anderson,' she said, oozing class. Nothing phased this dame. 'And I think I can use your talents.'

'Oh, a kneecap job,' he muttered. He hated those cheap assignments.

'Don't be stupid,' she said, a smile playing across her lips. 'If I'm gonna play Nemesis to someone who's stepped on the hem of my dress, I'm gonna get me a decent trigger man, not some two-bit bravo who cons farthings out of lonely old ladies.'

Fever hung his head. This lady didn't play by Queensberry rules.

'What I want,' she continued, 'is your dancing.'

Fever looked at her in amazement. 'Ya wanna dance with me?'

'Do I look as though I wanna go dancing, dumbhead?' Adèle tossed her sleek brown hair off her face, and fleetingly she looked surprisingly vulnerable. Maybe that was the moment she got under his skin. 'No, I figure I could help your career.'

'Are you an agent?' he gasped.

'No, but I'm willing to learn,' she said with authority. 'I've jazzed a bit myself, and I'm familiar with the club scene. I know the score, you might say. And anything I set my mind to, I do well.'

Fever looked at Adèle surlily. 'I don't want an amateur.'

A spasm of fury crossed her chiselled features. 'Right now, sonny boy, you should be grateful for a penny from a busker,' she rapped. 'And frankly, I haven't got time to waste persuading a no-account guy who doesn't know luck when it hits him over the head with a jemmy. I thought you had talent, but to succeed in showbiz you need brains as well. You obviously left yours in a locker room somewhere, buster.'

She rose to go, her face a mask of fury.

'Listen, I'm sorry,' said Fever hurriedly. 'Don't go. I . . . I don't know what's got into me. I'm just so deep in the gutter I can't even see as high as the step on the sidewalk. I need help and I can't even admit it to myself.'

Adèle paused in the doorway, staring at him searchingly. He went on, 'I just don't know what a classy dame like you would want with a piece of useless driftwood like me.'

'We're all in the gutter, but some of us are looking at the stars,' murmured Adèle, half to herself.

Fever looked blank.

'Guy named Wilde said that. Knew a lot about life, he did. Okay, let's talk.' Adèle walked back into the squalid closet he called a dressing-room. 'I think you've got talent.'

Fever looked at her disbelievingly. 'You don't know how well you dance,' she said, feasting her eyes on his Greek physique. 'Those hips . . . But you're lost in a line-up. You gotta go solo.'

'I've tried that,' he said wearily.

'Not the way I have in mind.' A suspicion of a smile hovered at the corners of her mouth. 'With your looks, your sense of rhythm, and that body, you could have thousands of women at your feet.'

'How do I do that?'

'Strip!' she snapped. 'Every women's sewing club up and down the land wants a male stripper for their annual party. You should see the acts they hire — they're dross. You and me, we'll work on an act, and I'll guarantee that you'll be the top paid strip artiste in the country in six months time. And don't go bashful on me. Anyone who spends most of their evenings wining and dining poor widows from East Cheam has to agree that stripping is a damn sight better way of earning a living.'

'Yeah,' he mumbled.

'What name do you work under?' she asked.

'Beau Dirkgarde,' he said with a touch of pride.

'It stinks,' she barked. 'From now on, you're Johnny Fever. And you can quit this hell-hole tonight.'

'Why are you doing this for me?' he asked, unsurely.

'Don't get me wrong — I'm not hooked on your personal charms. Let's just say I've taken a shine to you. And I like having people owe me a favour. Makes me feel good. Who knows when I might want you to do something for me.'

Fever remembered all this as clearly as if it was yesterday. And staring across the crowded bar, he thought ruefully of how right she'd been; now he *was* Johnny Fever, King of the Strips, idolised and desired by women all over England. He was her creation, her toy, and her success. But now he instinctively felt she was tiring — not of him, but of her whole life. She needed something new like an addict needs a fix.

That was the reason for coming to the Donmar tonight. He was returning her favour — literally. He had to get her on the stage. As yet, he wasn't sure how to go about that. But now she was waiting for him, so he downed the second bourbon quickly and made his way through the milling throng to where Adèle was sitting.

'What took you so long, big boy?' she said, but she was smiling. 'Fever, I want you to meet Gangland Frank, my escort for this evening.'

Fever nodded briefly to the fleshily handsome, well dressed man who sat beside his idol. He could never compete with a man like Gangland Frank: after all, Frank was a success in his own right. Frank wore diamonds; Frank had all the attributes he'd never have. It was ironic — Fever could have any woman but the one he most desired. Besides, this wasn't the Pygmalion story: Adèle wasn't going to fall in love with her own creation. Bernard Shaw got it right when he ruled out the happy ending.

'I've done all the research, Miss Anderson,' he said. 'This joint is run by a dame called Nica Burns, and it's her I have to approach.'

'Fine,' said Adèle. 'Get going, handsome.' She placed her delicate hand over Gangland Frank's big one. 'Frank's waiting to hear me sing.' She smiled at the big man in a way that twisted like a knife in Fever's heart, and then turned back to Fever, looking as distant as ever. He turned, and walked over to where the Spanish looking dame was standing.

For a tiny woman, Nica Burns packed a powerful punch. People watching her meteoric progress through the ranks of theatreland marked her down as someone to be admired, even feared. Only Nica knew how much she didn't know. She was still young, inexperienced, and masked it all under a veneer of brittle sophistication. But she was all too human, and when she saw Fever approaching her through the crowd, she felt her stomach turn over. This was one guy who could make her change her mind.

'Excuse me, you're Nica Burns, aren't you?'

She looked up at his tall frame. 'So what if I am, smartass?' This was one dame who could match Adèle blow for blow, even though Nica only came up to Adèle's waist.

'I just thought I ought to tell you that Miss Adèle Anderson is in the audience tonight, with a party of friends. And we'd very much like to hear her sing.'

Nica felt the prick of cold steel against her rib cage.

'Put it away,' she flashed, wearily. 'I don't buy threats.'

'I'm sorry. I was clumsy,' said Fever. His eagerness to help his mentor made him act stupidly. He pocketed the switchblade.

'That's fine,' said Nica. 'With looks like yours, handsome, you don't need to use violence. Tell your friend, I'll get her on the bill if I can. Okay?'

Nica's mind was racing. Who the hell was Adèle Anderson? The name sounded important, but she hadn't been in the business long enough to get to know everyone. Anyway, who cared if Adèle Anderson was some nobody — the crowd was in a mean mood tonight and would deal harshly with a bad singer. There was no need for her to get heavy, and besides, this dude had more than his fair share of naked sex-appeal, and Nica certainly appreciated that.

She went to the dressing room where the band were swigging moonshine and shooting up.

'Has any of you guys heard of a jazz singer, name of Adèle Anderson?'

They all looked blank, and Nica realised that though they were all in another world, where music was concerned they had their heads screwed on very firmly, and if they hadn't heard of this Anderson broad, she was a smart little nobody out on a very successful hustle. There'd be nothing and nobody these boys didn't know in the jazz world — after all, Nica herself had hand-picked the best jazz band in Europe.

So who was this Adèle Anderson? Oh well, no point in bothering her head about it now. She'd find out sooner or later. But the dude in the leather pants . . . now, he was something else . . . Yes, she'd make sure the Anderson broad sang, and then maybe she could get to talk to the guy again . . . yes . . .

Fever pushed his way back through the crush. 'It's all fixed,' he growled.

'Good boy,' purred Adèle. 'Frank will be very pleased. He likes you, Johnny.'

'Huh,' said Fever, concealing his anguish with a mask of indifference. 'Where is he, anyway?'

'He's in the little boys' room,' cooed the tall goddess. 'He has a few problems with his bladder.'

'Good,' thought Fever sourly.

Suddenly his reverie was interrupted. The stage lights came up, the band began to play a little louder, and the crowd cleared away from the stage area as a hush fell. On walked Bertice Reading, jazz singer extraordinaire. Boy, could she sing. She belted those songs out like she knew there was competition out there. Adèle would have to be very good indeed to stand up to that one. Fever had heard her sing in the toilet, but he had no idea whether she could sell herself.

At last, Bertice sang her final encore. The crowd didn't want to let her go, and roared for more. Then Nica appeared on the stage, and for a moment Fever thought she was going to bring Bertice back to do yet another number.

'Thank you, thank you,' said Nica, as the crowd fell silent once again. 'Ladies and Gentlemen, we have an unexpected surprise for you tonight. We're very lucky to have, in the audience, a performer of some note. I want you to welcome a jazz singer by the name of Adèle Anderson. Please, Ladies and Gentlemen, give her the applause she deserves. Miss Adèle Anderson!!!'

Adèle, looking momentarily surprised, rose from her seat and, with a soft smile at Fever, stepped gracefully into the spotlight as though born to it. A murmur ran through the crowd. They wanted Bertice, not some unknown, however stunning she was.

'Thank you,' she whispered, softly but surely. 'I'd like to sing to you now some old songs with new lyrics. I hope you like them.' Then she turned to the band, and after a few terse but clear instructions, ripped into a dazzling selection of standards.

Nica watched from the side as the lofty sex-kitten got the whole audience in the palm of her hand. Even the world weary drunks and the faded blondes at the bar turned from their tumblers of rye to watch the woman with the incredible voice and the risqué lyrics turn a howling mob into panting dogs. For a total newcomer, this Adèle Anderson sure had star quality. Then, out of the corner of her eye, Nica saw Fever's face, adoration suffusing his noble features. She smiled wryly to herself.

'You can't win 'em all, Burns,' she said under her breath, and went to the dressing room to await the new star.

At length, Adèle finished her set, and after a rapturous ovation swept backstage where Gangland Frank and his cronies were waiting with a crate of champagne. They all milled around her, kissing and hugging her, Frank standing with a proprietorial arm around her waist.

'Champagne for everybody!' called Frank, glowing with pride at his girl's success. Suddenly, a spasm of pain flashed across his florid face, and he rushed in the direction of the gents. Nica took the opportunity to go up to Adèle and stand squarely in front of her.

'I'm Nica Burns,' she said: 'I run this joint.'

'Yeah,' said Adèle, cool to the last.

'I direct a group called Fascinating Aïda.' Adèle shrugged her shoulders. She'd never heard of this outfit.

'They're a singing trio, and they're looking for a replacement,' continued Nica. 'They're good.'

'So?'

Nica looked Adèle straight in the eye. 'I'd like you to audition for them.'

In a flash, Adèle was transformed from Ice Princess to little girl.

'Really! Oh I'd love that!' she squealed. A legitimate job in showbiz? Any girl would kill for that.

Fever, watching the scene from the doorway, felt something die inside him. In a few seconds, he'd lost his woman, not to Gangland Frank, but to showbiz. Adèle was too good not to sail into this hick singing trio, whoever they were. They'd have to be halfwits not to employ her, and he reckoned Nica Burns was too smart a thinker to work with boneheads. Now there was some dame, he thought. In another time, another place . . . but his heart was Adèle's, and Adèle's heart was in showbiz.

He turned heavily, and went back to the hat check girl.

'Hi, Johnny!' she trilled. 'I'm free now. Wanna cut a rug with me?'

'Oh, hi Candy,' said Fever, only half in this world.

'Are we gonna boogie, Fever?' she lisped, pulling her tight dress down over her thighs in a manner that left most men weak with anticipation.

'No, Candy,' said Fever hollowly, 'not tonight.'

Candy saw the suffering in his face, and her hand reached out to touch his. 'A trouble shared . . .'

Fever smiled at her. She was a sweet girl under all the make-up. He shook his head in silent anguish.

Candy nodded. She understood. 'Okay, Johnny, but any time you need a friend . . .'

'Thanks, Candy,' he said softly, 'I won't forget. You're a very lovely girl.' Gently, he bent and kissed her on the lips, and a rosy blush spread over her doll-like face.

'Oh, Johnny . . . !' she said, but he had gone. He had slipped away into the night, a shadow among shadows, just another man looking for a place to hang his hat.

He was Johnny No-Name once more.

Johnny Fever wearing — yes — three pairs of tights, Queensland-style! All the surfers in Queensland, Australia, put on two pairs of tights on either end of their gorgeous bods over a bodystocking to protect themselves from the deadly whiplash of killer jellyfish!! (Note the natty hole cut in the gusset for eezi-head-thru effect!!!) Johnny goes one better and sports a toning swim-cap — it's no wonder all the girls love him!!!
Fashion Note: Say yes to Zig-zags!!!!!

MARILYN'S CROSSWORD

Across

1. Can be relied on for several 38 across (6)
5. There's F.A. tumbling down (8)
9. Potassium and grease compounded give short weight (4)
10. Lo, dried tip yields grain (4)
12. A good man has no truck with stills, considering them as misfortunes (4)
14. Sticks guess round novice with no direction (5)
16. Funny sound of bourbon (3)
17. Editing it out results in consent (5)
19. Chuck most of Irish hockey game (4)
22. Amorously eye duck, and the French surround note (4)
23. Golden orient trapped in this mineral (3)
24. A vest in charge presents musical intervals (7)
25. Hear a whinny? Never! (3)
28. Again, faint acids dissolve, leaving eponymous heroine(s) of the book (11, 4)
31. Stone quarry (3)
33. Orchestrate, and take no less from Sloane Rangers (7)
34. It pricks everything, we hear (3)
36. Memorial service renders nothing next to next to nothing (4)
38 A song for Ariadne without end (4)
39. Student in extra-sensory wrinkles (5)
41. Pluck bird from thigh bone (3)
42. Quietly tolled crash (5)
43. Penniless surfeit results in surfeit (4)
44. Grave decoration eaten by consumption (4)
45. 31 down. Secure Slavic cosmetic (4, 6)
46. Hello, slow down backwards with sex appeal and a second co-ordinate. Boisterous merriment (8)
47. A capital, a tick and almost a frown (6)

Down

1. Lightly dismiss U.S. city with an expression of distaste? Well! (5, 3)
2. Guarantee to follow round right (6)
3. Look out for supplements (4)
4. Abolish the king and instinctive impulses (3)
5. Parry for a month, about to find an agreeable combination? (4, 4, 7)
6. Type of junction, aged recounted (4)
7. Two points and a gesture denotes a standard (6)
8. Cartoonist could make a poet (or an ex-fiancé!) (6)
11. Fish may appear in fisherman's basket but without getting louder (3)
13. Blériot loses his pommie associations and emerges a king of beasts (3)
15. Extract the gas from 19 across and wind up an old trumpet (3)
18. A part of England, and of me (5)
20. Set special constable, I'm the eighth I am (7)
21. Oriental jade set in golfers' support is adolescent (7)
26. Perform diplomacy losing half a race (3)
27. Vehicle in front (3)
29. Bail I overturn for excuse (5)
30. Rosy, like 34 across silver down (3, 5)
31. See 45 across
32. Listen out for this tacky notion (6)
34. Some hear a bicycle, some hear a kind of gum (6)
35. Direction in gain (3)
37. Brew 43 across, but don't stir it with a pole (3)
38. Equip, rooted in 31 across (3)
40. Vermin back up for the main attraction (4)
42. Prolong without right direction or gravity is just a game (4)
44. Cut short duration for abbreviated boy's name (3)

Answers on page 156

MY DREAM MAN

Ev'ry girl goes through a phase of having some kind
  of idol:
He's the one she dreams about when feeling
  suicidal:
From Bogart through to Superman, I've admired a
  few:
But I've acquired a new pin-up, who I'll reveal to
  you . . .

I fancy the Pope:
Yes he's my current fad:
I might seem a dope
But he reminds me of my Dad.
Oh he's so warm and fatherly
There's nowhere else I'd rather be
Than down in the crowd at the Holy See:
Yes, I fancy the Pope.

I'm pots about the Prelate,
Yes, he's the pearl in my oyster:
I'm a potential zealot
So please take me to his cloister.
He travels abroad on many trips
So that with the world's problems he can get to
  grips:
How I wish I were the ground beneath his lips
Yes I fancy the Pope.

Now certainly I don't intend to shock, or to
  blaspheme:
But when it comes to other heroes, ooh that man's a
  dream.

While speaking eighteen languages he never talk
  baloney:
He's great and good, he's wise and strong, yes he
  the real polony:

I fancy the Pope
He makes my knees go trembly:
I nurture the hope
That he'll come back to Wembley.
If I met him I don't know what I'd do:
'Cos the words he speaks are good and true
And what's more, he's infallible too
Yes I fancy the Pope.

I'm mad about the Pontiff
He makes my heart beat quicker:
I doubt if I could quantify
My feelings for this vicar.
I realize that the average gel
Won't understand quite how I fell:
It was when I found out he writes plays as well
Yes I fancy the Pope

Oh I've got a picture on my wall
Of Karol Wojtyla — alias Pope John Paul
But he could only ever love me as a sister, that's
Yes I fancy the
Fancy schmancy the
I fancy the Pope
Oy vey.

Words and Music by Dillie Kea
Additional lyrics by Adèle Anders

CHAPTER NINE

MISS ANDERSON SAVES THE DAY

Nica was by now running the Donmar Warehouse Theatre in Covent Garden: she'd met Ian Albery at the same Edinburgh Festival that we had, and he'd obviously been more impressed with her than with us because he'd offered her the job of Artistic Director. She was beginning to make a large number of contacts in the cabaret world and drew up an audition list consisting of people who'd either been recommended through the business or who'd performed at the Donmar.

She went through the list with us. 'I've got one girl who's a *fantastic* impersonator – does impressions of Streisand, Minnelli and Piaf – and another extraordinary girl with a wonderful voice called Adèle Anderson who bluffed her way into singing after Bertice's show the other night.'

Nica, Marilyn and I held auditions in my flat – in my bedroom, to be precise, for my piano lives as near to my hands as possible – and the short list narrowed down quickly to these two. Adèle certainly was dramatic: we had no idea what to make of her other than that she was tremendously musical. She arrived at my flat wearing a calf-length, rust coloured raincoat and a matching hat with the brim pulled well down over one eye – she looked as though she was auditioning for Mata Hari. Underneath, she wore a knee-length, blue-grey knitted dress covered in bobbly bunches of red grapes; her hair was cut in a Louise Brookes bob and she seemed gigantic in her high heels. She was an unusual vision.

Then she sang for us, and I shall never forget it. She placed the music in front of me and I started to play the song which was, I recall, in E♭. I nearly fell off my stool when she sang the whole thing an octave lower.

'What's your range?' I asked in amazement when she'd got through the song.

Instead of answering 'D below Middle C to top B♭' like most people would, she opened her mouth as wide as it could go, emitted a low growl somewhere in the region of the Bass E♭ and went up the scale to Top C – nearly five octaves. It was not a heavenly noise but it sure was impressive.

Anyone that eccentric endears themselves to me immediately, and we got chatting: she wanted to know about the group and we needed to know more about her. I asked her if she'd join me in a glass of cooking sherry and was reassured when she knocked it back – one teetotaller in a group is quite enough. There was, however,

Adèle relives the day of her audition in that *dress. Today Fascinating Aïda,
tomorrow La Traviata?*

something odd about her, something slightly bizarre. She seemed to
be an anachronism, and reminded us of the pre-war cabarets of
Berlin. Her height and her basso profundo voice puzzled us.

At last Nica voiced the awful question. 'Adèle, I have to ask you
something,' she said awkwardly. 'Are you a man?' It wasn't a subtle
way of asking her, but how the hell can you be subtle about
something like that?

Adèle went pink and looked mortified and wounded, as though
we'd asked her if she was a thief or a sneak.

'No,' she said after a moment, so obviously hurt by the question
that we felt embarrassed we'd even thought it in the first place. And
we were then fairly satisfied that she wasn't nor ever had been a
man: she was just a tall woman with a deep voice.

We called her for a second audition and it was a straight choice between her and the impressionist, who was a tiny, dark girl with a pixie face and lots of talent. She wasn't right for us, we felt, but she'd have a good career very soon if she followed her own star. We were right – her name was Jessica Martin.

We decided unanimously that Adèle was to be our third member. We had no doubts that she was the right choice: somehow she completed the picture. There was an instant rapport that we hadn't found with anyone else, and her singing blended perfectly with ours.

Of course, as we later found out, Adèle was a transsexual. She went home and agonised with her flatmate Stevan over whether to tell us. Eventually, she took his advice and stayed silent, feeling that if she got the job it would be on her merits and that knowing the truth would cloud our eyes to her talent. And I don't know if we would have chosen her if we'd known: transsexuals don't get a great press and I'm not sure we'd have been that brave. I'm glad now we didn't know, because we were never faced with that dilemma and chose her simply because she was right. As she herself said, she was the best man for the job.

Adèle's version ...

When Dillie rang me to say I'd got the job my heart leapt and almost immediately sank like a stone. This was an all-girl group I was about to join. Did the fact that I was a transsexual automatically disqualify me? I consulted several friends, all of whom said, 'Certainly not. For many years you've lived as a woman and worked as a woman and been accepted as a woman. Why should you view this job differently from any other?' They were naïvely supportive, bless them, for of course none of them could foresee just how successful Fascinating Aïda would become, with the accompanying press interest that entailed.

My own reasoning was this: I was by no means the only girl to have auditioned and so the fact that I had been chosen meant that Dillie, Marilyn and Nica considered me to be the right person for the job. Deep down, I suspected that if I 'revealed all', they would be unable to see beyond my transsexualism, particularly as they hardly knew me. I'd learnt, from one or two past boyfriends, that if a person got to know and like me without being aware of my past, when they subsequently found out it was unimportant. However, if they knew upon meeting me that I was transsexual their prejudices, conscious or unconscious, immediately threw up barriers between us. And anyway, I was to be employed on a three month trial basis. I might not gel with Marilyn and Dillie for a number of reasons —

vocally, personally or professionally. In short, given my lack of theatrical experience, I might prove to be no good at all and be given the push. In which case that would be two more relative strangers walking around who'd know my life history and I didn't want that.

Sometimes being a transsexual can feel like being an ex-prisoner. You finished your sentence years ago and yet you are never allowed to forget that once you spent time inside. There are members of the public who feel that's right — you should never be allowed to forget — but I don't subscribe to that viewpoint. I paid my debt to society with the twenty years I was forced to spend as a male and I don't wish to be constantly reminded of it. (Nor do I wish to discuss it at parties with total strangers. Funny how surprised people get when I turn stroppy because they want to know the intimate details of my sex life!) Since I shall spend the rest of my life living as a female I do not see why I should have to set myself apart from other women and think of myself as 'second-class'. I've had a gutful of apologising for doing my damnedest to conform to 'normal' society. The fact is, I have now succeeded in taking my place in it and have something to give to it as well. I feel I should be allowed to do so without others pointing the finger.

So much for tub thumping. As Fitz says, 'Nobody loves a cross girl', and I'm sure Dillie and Marilyn would have been appalled if I'd tried to bully them into taking me on regardless. So I kept quiet, let them get to know me, and waited to see what would happen.

It was difficult to keep a balance at first. Adèle was eager to prove herself as a lyricist and kept bringing me her latest offerings. She'd impressed us with her outrageous parodies of standard songs, but this was different. For a start, her topics were completely wrong for the group, and secondly she was writing lyrics without any shape in mind.

A lyricist must have an understanding of music, form and rhythm. A songwriter (i.e. someone who writes both words and music) can be completely untrained as she can translate her concept into song without having the slightest knowledge of musical conventions. A lyricist, on the other hand, *must* be musically well-versed because she has to be able to communicate her concept of form and rhythm to her collaborator, otherwise the tunesmith will not be able to understand her intentions. It's all very well being able to parody the words of an extant song: that's relatively easy because the original writer has done all the groundwork and the architecture of the song is there for the parodist to burgle. It's another thing entirely to create your own shape and verse form. It can be done without years

Our first official snaps with Adèle, taken by the wonderful Michael Mayhew, who captured perfectly the quirkiness of the group.

of training and some people do have a natural gift for it, but all the best lyricists studied, studied, studied, familiarising themselves with techniques, immersing themselves in the work of other lyricists and analysing why song lyrics work.

Adèle produced lyric after lyric: all unworkable and unsingable. Now she looks back and laughs at her early efforts, but at the time I had to go very carefully and encourage her through constructive criticism – 'tread carefully, for you tread on my dreams'. And it has paid off because she has become a fine lyricist.

Our approach to the job of writing the song lyrics has changed. At first, we all tried to write them. Then it became clear that each of us had different strengths. Marilyn, for instance, was always the commission supremo. Unlike Adèle or me, she is a highly organised person who likes to know in advance what she's doing. The commissions suited her because she could plan to set a day aside for writing the song. Her academically trained brain then sorted through the various approaches to a subject: she researched widely, sifted through her own enormous store of knowledge, and would finally hit on the most appropriate and interesting angle. On the other hand, Adèle and I usually take it in turns to go blank on the commissions, and are only sporadically of any use. Yet, when we're writing commissions, they are almost always best when co-written.

The rest of our songs come out of the blue and I have tended to write these mainly by myself: if I have a very clear notion of what the song is going to be about, it only dilutes the idea to share it. If I get stuck, I then call in the others. At the beginning, Marilyn used to enjoy joining in on the writing of non-commissioned songs (she co-wrote 'Herpes' and 'Bunker Lullaby') but as FA's work increased and ate up more and more of our private life, she began to get protective about her free time. When Adèle joined the group, she and I always travelled to gigs together as Marilyn had to leave earlier to do the lighting, and this became a habit. Even when we had a tour manager and all travelled in the van, Marilyn would sleep in the back on a futon as she gets travel sick. So Adèle and I were naturally thrown together more, and I started to discuss my ideas with her. Her approach had become less aggressive and more sophisticated and oblique. Nowadays, we constantly collaborate on my ideas, and she contributes ideas of her own.

I'm dreadfully neurotic: every time I write a song, I'm certain it's my last. It's not that I think the tunes will run out – just the ideas. I've written or co-written about eighty songs in three years so perhaps I'm worrying about nothing. But as the group gets more successful, so the pressures increase and there is less time to write, less time even to think. I try to lay aside free time, but there's always something that crops up that steals the days away – interviews, photo sessions, letters to answer, business lunches to eat. All of which apparently futile activities are vitally necessary to the life of the group.

Demarcation has been our motto ever since Adèle joined. Marilyn deals with all things technical i.e. lighting and sound; Adèle is archivist, secretary and now project co-ordinator, and I'm in charge of money, the law and negotiations. I'm much more vociferous than the others, and I was much in demand as a legal secretary during my temping days, so contracts have always been my department. This means I've been lumbered with the rôle of group virago as Adèle and Marilyn simply don't want to deal with that side of things: they find it daunting and confusing. On the other hand, I'm not consistent enough to do the regular donkey work, so what we call the Jack

One of the first gigs with Adèle, and the only time a guitar ever appeared on stage. It was not a success (the guitar, not the gig).

Sprat factor comes into effect – we lick the platter clean by virtue of our differing abilities and likes.

The most important thing in a group is that everybody should feel that they have something to contribute. It's no good having two writing and one idle. The third person will inevitably end up feeling discontented and unwanted.

So apart from initial problems with writing, Adèle settled into the group as though born to it. And for the first time I had a pal who liked doing the same things as I did, i.e. drinking and socialising and eating at the Little Chef. My friendship with Marilyn thrived on the differences between us: Adèle and I used our similarities to forge a strong bond. Adèle and Marilyn, while being as different as it is possible for two people to be, formed the perfect working relationship based on mutual respect but they never socialised outside work.

However, Marilyn was beginning to feel openly dissatisfied with Fascinating Aïda: she was getting offers of acting work and was unhappy about turning them down – Fascinating Aïda had been working full time from the days of the Dublin Theatre Festival. She always admitted openly that she couldn't help feeling the work we were doing to be somehow inferior to straight theatre: after all, it was only 'cabaret'. I, being a deeply neurotic and over-sensitive creature, reacted badly to this. I felt it was a slight on my work, whereas with hindsight I can see that her feelings were prompted by the fact that she was simply not in the right milieu. She enjoyed a great deal of the work we were doing, especially writing to commission, but she was a square peg in a round hole. I couldn't understand that she was simply not a Vaudevillian and never would be, whereas Adèle and I were. And this caused the first cracks in our friendship.

Things progressed smoothly. We were taken on by a new agency more suited to our line of work called, improbably, Hetherington Seelig. Adèle and I took Michelle, our agent, out to lunch and told her that we were going to look for a variety agent, and about two weeks later had to take her out to lunch again to tell her we'd found one. She was both sad and relieved: she'd said many times that she was only our caretaker because variety was not her speciality, but she put in a lot of hard work on our behalf and was a good friend.

What had happened was this: Rachel Swann, who worked for Hetherington Seelig, had been tentatively putting out feelers towards another music cabaret group: they got quite a long way in their negotiations, and then the group decided that they were happy with their existing arrangement after all. This left Rachel high, dry, and raring to go. Shortly after, Nica met Rachel at the Donmar and persuaded her to come and see us, and within a few days we were meeting to discuss representation. Rapport was definitely oozing from the ozone that day, because it was one of those 'gosh, isn't everybody nice' meetings. Joseph Seelig and Stephen Hetherington were funny and charming, and Rachel was clearly a gift from above.

It's vitally important to like your agent. In my career as an actress, I had a total of three agents and I never felt at all comfortable with any of them. The relationship between performer and agent is monstrously difficult, especially when the performer is out of work. If the agent is a good and caring one, he/she may feel worried and guilty that their client is sitting at home (or out temping) utterly miserable, demoralised and broke. The client can be one of those neurotic types who ring their poor agents every single day without fail to find out if there are any offers or auditions.

I was the opposite type. I'd sit at home chewing my nails, cursing whichever luckless agent was supposedly representing me at that time, feeling embarrassed that I was out of work and too afraid to ring and find out that, yet again, there was nobody in the whole wide world interested in employing D. Keane.

It wasn't until Michelle started looking after Fascinating Aïda's business that I realised what a tough job being an agent is, and I don't think enough actors give their agents credit for the amount of slog, heartbreak and, frequently, love that is poured out on their behalf. I'd sit in Michelle's office goggling at her tireless patience and doggedness as she tried to persuade producers, directors and casting directors to employ her clients. And when her efforts were fruitless, I was sorry for her because some of the clients made it clear that they didn't think she was trying hard enough for them.

Of course there are terrible agents who do nothing for their clients and are quite content to cream off their ten or fifteen percent even when you've got the job through your own efforts. In that case it's better not to have an agent at all, but a lot of performers think it's such a stigma not to have an agent that they resign themselves to putting up with dross: a mistake, I think.

But it's an even bigger mistake to expect your agent to be able to work miracles. You've got to get off your butt and look for work yourself in this business. If you're too much of a slob or too proud to go job hunting on your own, then you deserve to be unemployed. An agent is there to help and advise you and to make sure you don't get lumbered with an appalling contract, not to wipe your bum for you.

Since starting Fascinating Aïda with Lizzie and Marilyn, we've been lucky to have been represented by people we like and trust, but we've always not only wiped our own bums but done all our own laundry. We don't demand miracles.

Four months after Adèle joined us, the bomb dropped. A friend of mine that I hadn't seen in years turned up at a charity show we did at the Piccadilly Theatre, and it transpired that she'd also met Adèle some years before. She rang me the next day to say how much she'd enjoyed our act, and went on to talk about the personalities of the group.

'It's fascinating to see how you all work together,' she said, 'because you're all so different. And Adèle adds a marvellously bizarre element, I suppose, because she was a man.'

I had to hold on to the telephone table, but I managed to keep my cool till the end of the conversation. My initial response was anger: anger at Adèle's deception; anger at being made to feel a fool. We'd asked her at the audition, and accepted her denial as fact.

But after I thought about it a little more I realised that everything fell into place. I'd always had my suspicions but I had dismissed them, preferring to believe the easier option. I can only liken it to the shock you get when, although you've known in your heart that someone is dying, they do actually die.

In a state of bewilderment, I called Marilyn and she was as taken aback as I'd been. We discussed the implications, especially with regard to the kind of prurient press coverage we were likely to receive, but neither of us had any idea of how to cope with such a thing – it was completely beyond our middle-class comprehension.

'Let's go and talk to Nica,' said Marilyn, when we could reach no satisfactory conclusion.

Nica's reaction to the news was nonchalant, to say the least. 'Oh really?' she said. 'So what?'

We mumbled something about problems in the future. 'Are you suggesting that we should sack her?' demanded Nica with a glint in her eye.

'Of course not,' we said hastily, shifting about uncomfortably in our seats.

'Good, because she does the job we asked her to do and does it well, and that's all that matters,' said Nica. 'Her past has nothing to do with anything. You certainly can't blame her for what she's done. In fact, I have nothing but the highest regard for her.'

And that was that.

But there was still the problem of finding a way to communicate to Adèle that we knew her secret without making a confrontation out of it. We accepted it and wanted to support her, but the 'I-know-and-I-know-that-you-don't-know-that-I-know' situation was most disquieting. It was just like being at a large dinner party and noticing that someone you've just met has lettuce on their teeth: you have no idea how to tell them and every time you look at them all you can see or think of is lettuce, lettuce, lettuce.

A couple more months passed and no opportunity presented itself.

Then up at the Edinburgh Festival, the second bombshell dropped, this time on poor Adèle's head. We were playing to packed houses at the Assembly Rooms: reviewers were unanimously raving about us and we were riding on the crest of a ripple. Then, just before the show one evening, Nica showed Marilyn and me a review that had appeared in the *Financial Times* that day written by Michael Coveney:

> 'It is worth fighting through the Assembly Rooms, knapsacks and mohican hairdos, to see Fascinating Aïda, a talented trio of singers who put the skids under Sloane Rangers. One of the girls, Adèle, has a wonderfully smoky voice and could fool me that she was a slinky transvestite. There is a wonderfully witty song about falling in love with the Pope and a splendid Liza Minnelli spoof in a sneak preview number from an upcoming musical version of *The Three Sisters*. Look out Moscow, here they come.'
>
> *Tuesday, 28th August, 1984.*

Yes, it was as complimentary as we could have desired, but 'slinky transvestite'? Knowing the truth, it seemed unnecessarily cruel. We rushed into the dressing room, and discovered Adèle sobbing her heart out.

'It's all right, Adèle,' said Marilyn hugging her. 'We know. And as far as we're concerned, it doesn't matter a damn. What's more, you *are* a woman, and we think you're very brave.'

And there the matter rested for a good while longer.

CHAPTER TEN

GET KNOTTED

Hard on the heels of a wildly successful Festival came the recording and publishing contracts. For a heady month or so it was dotted lines a-gogo and they were pretty irresistible. Of course, being the sensible, grown-up women we are, we took hefty legal advice and only autographed these contracts after we were completely satisfied that our short and curlies were well protected. Unfortunately, what we didn't realise is that while we could guard ourselves till kingdom come against the sharks making a grand for every half pence we earned, it didn't defend us against the preconceptions of our assignors.

Fascinating Aïda were signed up to make a single and an album with BBC Records. Right from the word go we were enthusiastic about the album, and the single was just a bit of fun whose chances of succeeding roughly approximated Leon Brittan's chances of getting into the Bolshoi. Still, given that Joe Dolce and Orville the Duck had each had a big hit in recent years, we thought it was worth having a go at releasing one of our sillier songs, and anyway, BBC Records insisted on making a single as they said it would boost sales of the album. So we signed the contract assuming that it couldn't possibly do us any harm.

What we didn't realise was that this was BBC Records' first attempt at capturing the pop market with a record not allied to a TV programme. They'd had hits in the past (with Orville the Duck and the songs from *Fame*, for example), but more by virtue of the popularity of the programme than forward planning. Our reason for going with them was simple: while we'd had interest expressed by other companies, we felt that BBC Records would take us as we were and wouldn't try to change us. Ha!

Our first planning meeting was one of the most frustrating experiences of my life. The moguls were clearly putting us in our places. We were told we were ignorant of current trends, and that they were looking for a pop sound: our songs were too clever, our image was an old-fashioned mess, we desperately needed revamping under their guidance, and we should change our name permanently to Sweet FA as Fascinating Aïda was far too intellectual for mere record buyers to comprehend. By this time, we had an extremely clear idea of who and what we were and the notion that our songs were too clever for the 57 million people in the UK was, in our view, patronising both to us and to our potential audience.

We argued that we were not a pop group, never would be and

One of the Brian Aris photographs. We were very lucky to get such a wonderful photographer, and it must be said that BBC Records did us proud with the official snaps.

furthermore had no aptitude for it. Then we tried making the point that we didn't think that BBC Records was really a pop label.

'Ah, but BBC Records is in the middle of a momentous change of direction,' was the gist of the reply. 'And we won't consider making the album without making a pop single first.'

Aghast, we bucked and reared, and tried to explain that we were a quirky little outfit with an acoustic sound and were happy that way. To no avail. They had us on a snaffle bit and we had to produce a song that fitted their requirements – no gags, and a painfully simple tune.

So we couldn't win or find a compromise, and the most absurd thing of all was that it transpired they'd signed us up without having come to see the act.

What the moguls wanted was a product, not people. They thought we'd be delighted to be moulded into a poor woman's Bucks Fizz, but all they got was three ungrateful women quite content as they were.

We sank into utter dejection. Our talent was little enough, God knows, but it was all we had and when we saw it being diluted, it was very painful. Fascinating Aïda had consumed a year and a half of Marilyn's and my lives, which isn't that much, but to have our work treated this way was extremely distressing. An artist can only do well what she does from the heart: enforced change debases the coinage.

We mooted our song about tights as a contender. 'There's always room for a novelty single,' said Marilyn.

'Too clever,' said the moguls. 'We've played it to our secretaries, and they didn't understand it.'

'What do they wear? Pop socks?' I asked.

'Write a pop song,' they commanded. We tried, with not a lot of success. Eventually we wrote a song called 'Wallies'.

> Verse: What a load of wallies,
>   Wallies ev'rywhere:
>   They get up my nostrils,
>   And they get in my hair.
>   They cause aggravation:
>   Wallies are the pits,
>   They get underneath my skin
>   And they get on my nerves.
>
> Chorus: Wallies, bloomin' wallies,
>   Spike them with your brollies.
>   They get my goat but not my vote:
>   Oy, oy, oy! bloomin' wallies.

'Wallies' was rejected. I went to meet Bruce Talbot, our producer, who was by far the most sympathetic of the staff that we'd met thus far. We sat and discussed the problem – it was clear that he was caught between two stools. He had a job to do, but wanted to represent us in a way that we'd be happy with. I sang him all the songs he hadn't heard so far, and eventually dredged up 'Get Knotted'.

'That's the one,' he said with limited enthusiasm. 'It's certainly the nearest to what we're looking for.'

So 'Get Knotted' it was.

We suggested that our friend Steve Riffkin do the arrangement. We'd met him with The Brass Band in Edinburgh. He'd done a lot of their arrangements and we liked him a great deal: what's more he was American and had all the right musical credentials. Unfortunately he had the impossible task of turning a cotton purse into a sow's ear, and while the arrangement he wrote was impressive, we simply felt that the idea was so wrongheaded in the first place that whatever he did was bound to fail. It was so magnificently produced that you couldn't recognise us. Instead of sounding like the gin-soaked though mellifluous old trouts we are (pace Marilyn who is TT), we sounded like Manhattan Transfer singing underneath a tin tub.

The thing that most distressed us was how badly we had to behave (and it was mostly me who had the tantrums) to nice people – for ironically they are – to make them see that all they did was make us unhappy, and the more they robbed us of our identity, the less likely we were to produce good work. I behaved like a harridan, and I didn't much like myself.

'Write it all off to experience,' we agreed, depressed.

Then in the middle of all this brouhaha, dear old overworked St. Jude stepped in on our behalf. We had a phone call from Mark Chapman, the director who'd done the Health Farm documentary the previous year and who'd used our songs. He explained that he was directing another documentary for *Forty Minutes* and had been in the middle of making one about air hostesses when British Airways decided not to let him film their girls when they were off duty.

'But there'll be no story!' said Mark, horrified.

'Sorree!' said British Airways. End of documentary.

Mark was frantic. He only had a few weeks left to set up, film and edit a completely new story, he'd used up part of his budget already and had several days filming in the can which were now wasted. He was sitting at a table in conference with Roger Mills, the series producer, feeling thoroughly downcast and trying to think of a new topic when Roger came up with an idea.

'What about those girls who did the singing for you last year?' he asked.

'Oh, Fascinating Aïda?' said Mark.

'Yes. Why don't you find out what's happened to them? Perhaps there's a story there.'

So Mark phoned us to find out what we were doing.

'Oh Mark!' we wailed, 'it's all *awful!*' and told him the whole ghastly story of the deadlock with BBC Records. (BBC Records, it should be said, is an entirely separate department from BBC Television.) He expressed a cautious interest and came down to see us at the studio. Within a couple of days the whole thing was set up. We would receive a modest fee for our participation, and BBC Records agreed to co-operate and let us and themselves be filmed in the process of making our single.

Mark decided that the film wouldn't be complete without being able to show the original production meeting, so we had to set it up again. Accordingly, everyone showed up at BBC Records to recreate it as accurately as possible. Cameras rolled, Mark said 'Go!', and we started to talk about the single. To my absolute horror the moguls were being very low-key now that the cameras were there. I was incensed, and after about twenty minutes, I leapt out of my seat.

'This is outrageous!' I shouted, weeping with vexation. 'You're not saying any of the things you said at the first meeting.'

'What do you mean?' asked one executive, looking innocent.

'You've softened everything. Last time you said our songs were too clever, but you said we should use synthesisers, you said we were out of date and needed revamping, boo hoo . . .'

I turned to Mark. 'This is terrible, Mark. They're changing everything.'

Mark calmed me down, and with infinite tact got the scene rolling again. Eventually, of course, he managed to film enough material that showed in some measure the extent to which BBC Records wanted to change our style, and it was one of the most memorable scenes in the documentary. The line 'What's wrong with being patronising if it makes money?' was much remarked upon by our many correspondents after the film was shown.

Mark and his team followed us around for about three weeks, coming to the Belfast Arts Festival too. It was exhausting work: we were filming all day and doing the late show at night, and Adèle and I found the Northern Irish socialising irresistible so we were always hung over. And as Mark is a perfectionist the filming was often wearing and repetitive. But by the end, we all had such great respect for him that we'd have walked over hot coals for him. We didn' know if he sympathised with us or not: we simply knew he wanted to make a good, truthful documentary.

And the thing that impressed us most of all was that although Mark knew at the time of filming about Adèle's secret, he never used it in the film as others might have done in similar circumstance in order to make the story more sensational. He felt that not only was it irrelevant to our work, but also that Adèle was entitled to her privacy. It's not often one has the privilege of working with a truly honourable person.

To be fair, it wasn't all bad at BBC Records. After all, they took the arranger we wanted in an effort to be accommodating. And as far as the actual production of the single and the design of the cover, we had absolutely no criticism: Bruce, the producer, and Mario, the art director, did the best they possibly could, but they hadn't a chance.

The single was timed to come out in the same week as the documentary, i.e. late January 1985. That week was extremely fraught First we had the record launch to get through. It was held at the Donmar Warehouse, and to our intense mortification, we were ordered by BBC Records to perform. We had to do fifteen minute of our own acoustic songs as per normal, then 'Get Knotted' would be played over the sound system, and we'd mime to it. We protested

Adèle demonstrates some imaginative ways of disposing of your least favourite singles. L-R: Attractive letter rack; Handy clip-on directo-lite (attach it to your hand for greater flexibility); Unusual pot-plant holder; Two exotic coasters. Fashion Note — Adèle's earrings are segments of a disc.

that this was ridiculous and that we'd look like pratts leaping about with microphones pretending to sing to a non-existent full orchestra. But there was no getting out of it. So I suggested we use three plastic roses to sing into instead of microphones and send the whole thing up. Nica choreographed us, and we did a very silly dance routine, miming all the instruments and singing out of synch with the words, so it wasn't quite as ghastly as it could have been.

The next day we went up to Birmingham to be interviewed on Pebble Mill about the documentary which was to be shown that night. BBC Records had rung us in high anxiety: I couldn't be relied upon to keep my trap shut and had already vexed the moguls with an article I wrote in *Time Out* about how unhappy we were. The documentary had aroused quite a lot of interest and was pick of the day in three major newspapers, and all the previewers had recommended it, drawing special attention to the way it exposed the pop business. The reviewer for *The Times* waxed furious and called it 'a murder story: Death by crass commercialism.'

So the moguls commanded us that we were under no circum-stances to say that we didn't like the record: we were there simply to plug it. Nobody gets anywhere by ordering us about, though, and

after all, we'd been honest with them from the start and were fed-ι
with the whole damn charade.

Of course, the interviewer, Paul Coia, asked us whether we lik
the record, and we tried very hard not to be damning but it w
impossible to be polite about such a piece of garbage. At one poii
I became quite incensed, when Paul understandably pointed o
that other acts would think we were being ungrateful.

'Yes,' I said bridling, 'it's a case of biting the hand that feeds yo
But if the hand that feeds you is that hand that chains you, do y
blame the bear for biting back? Come on! we're performing bea
that's all we are. We're signed, with a contract, and we had no sa

Then Marilyn compounded the felony by saying she thought t
record was bland. BBC Records were none too delighted with ι
Poor men: as Marilyn remarked in the documentary, they'd certain
got a pig in a poke when they took us on. And lest anyone thinks I'
simply knocking them, it was a completely different story when
came to making the album – they went out of their way to try ai
represent us as we wished. As I said on the back of the album, ν
loved every minute of the process of making it and we dedicat
'Moscow' to Bruce Talbot, our producer, and Ian Hughes, o
arranger, for working themselves to a frazzle and making the whc
project such fun.

Yes, BBC Records came good. But what of EMI, our publisher
We had wanted to go with another publisher, but BBC have a
arrangement with EMI and we were told our records wouldn't I
made unless we signed with EMI. They drove a hard bargain, payi
us 50% of our performing royalties (they're not allowed to pay
any less) for ten years. They wanted to charge us a royalty f
including some of the songs in this book – hence the absence of *T
Herpes Tango* etc. (I suppose we'd have got 50% of that mon
back, but it doesn't feel right having to pay for your own songs to I
published.) And they have yet to prove to me the advantage
having a publishing contract at all.

The documentary was broadcast that night and within ten days ν
were receiving a huge number of letters from all over the plac
Only one lady complained at our use of rude words: she was ve
upset that she'd recommended us to her friends having heard us c
Stop The Week, but the rest were decidedly for us.

'*Please please* don't let anyone persuade you to change yo
image.'

'Keep fighting to do your own thing.'

...Y MINUTES — SWEET F.A.
(... 2) may have disappointed
...rs expecting a programme
...t football.

...ut for me this showcase for
...stylish, witty girls' singing trio
...inating Aïda was a highspot of
...viewing week.

...Dillie Keane, Marilyn Cutts and
...e Anderson have a combination of

gifts I would have thought
impossible — fashionable
good looks, songwriting
ability and the black
humour of Tom Lehrer.
Even when driving down
the motorway the rhyming
couplets trip from their
lips.

Apart from the pleasure of
their stage act, I enjoyed the
cynical sub-plot of their relationship with BBC Records.

who are apparently not connected with the BBC crew
making the documentary. It
seemed one section of the
Corporation was making fun
of the other.

Girls

For the BBC Records
people who had signed the
girls without seeing their
stage show were now dubious
about their repertoire. They
wanted something "the girls

in the office" would understand.

The song which was finally
recorded—called Get Knotted
—was released this week. To
me it sounds like the Andrews
Sisters with the wrong lyrics
sheet.

Marilyn summarised : "It's
a beautiful production, but it
isn't anything to do with us."
Adele, who always seems to
have the last word, added
glumly "It'll be a hit in life
all over Britain—"

I hope this television
exposure will do as much for
Sweet Aïda as The Bigtime
did for Sheena Easton.

*The Daily Express,
2nd February 1985*

● I don't know what **SWEET F.A.**
(BBC 2, 9.30pm) started out as, but
what it ends up as is a murder story.
Death by crass commercialism:
steamroller conformity flattening out
individuality. Mark Chapman's film
is, however, a murder yarn with an
important difference. This victim
survives. Or rather, the victims do,
for the foul deed is perpetrated
against a trio, Dillie Keane, Marilyn
Cutts and Adèle Anderson who,
jointly, make up the singing group
known as Fascinating Aïda, and
there is an abundance of evidence
in *Sweet F.A.* to suggest that they
have sufficient talent, energy and
guts (the triumvirate are not
squeamish about sounding
physical, so why should I be?) not
only to live to fight another day, but
to win triumphantly. But enough of
metaphors. What tonight's *Forty
Minutes* documentary does is to

show what happened when a BBC
record company, realizing that there
was money to be made out of
Fascinating Aïda in view of their
stage, radio and television success,
got them to make a disc. What they
signally failed to realize was that the
Misses Keane, Cutts and Anderson,
plus Miss Keane's piano, make a
complete statement. Theirs is the
cabaret circuit Alpha and Omega.
They write all their own songs
(astonishingly varied ditties ranging
from plaintive songs like the one
about time and youth to scatological
numbers like the herpes tango), and
they sound like nobody else. The
BBC recording team, beady eyes on
the pop market, swung into action.
A mediocre song (the BBC's
choice), instead of a mordant one

(the girls' choice). Out went Miss
Keane's eloquent piano and the
trio's natural rhythm. In came a big
band, and spectacular syncopation.
Suddenly, Fascinating Aïda became
latter-day Andrews Sisters. They
had become homogenised, and it is
a disillusioned, but presumably
wiser, trio we see holding a post-
mortem towards the end of tonight's
film.

Peter Davalle

The Times, 2nd February 1985

Women are the best comedians on the
box at the moment, too, from the ageless
Felicity Kendall in Carla Lane's bitter-
sweet The Mistress (BBC2, Thursdays, 9
pm) to down-to-earth Victoria Wood
(BBC2, Fridays, 9 pm). The new generation of women comics is by preference
raunchy and none more so than Fascinating Aïda. They are also vulnerable, as
Forty Minutes — Sweet FA (BBC2, 24
January) made clear. This was an odd
inter-departmental effort, as one part of
the BBC filmed another — the record-
producing part — ineptly trying to find a
hit single among the songs of these three
witty young women. The women came
across as clever and honest, but the junk-
minded nitwits who work for BBC Records, probably think "originality" is the
name of a wine-bar in the King's Road.

The Tablet, 2nd February 1985

*A supportive letter in
the Radio Times, and
no, it wasn't from
Dillie's mum. We're still
waiting for that series.*

Fascinating 'Forty Minutes'

Fascinating Aïda is the most original
group to appear on BBCtv for years
(Forty Minutes, 24 January BBC2). I
think they were marvellous. They have
a lot to say about a lot of subjects. I
agree with what the group was saying
about the attempts to turn them into
pop stars – they aren't. It portrays the
wrong image of them by trying to make
them so Please don't lose them – their
satire is too precious. Give their talent
full rein and give them a series.

Warwick, Cumbria   (Mrs) B.M. Keen

THEY ASK FOR THE
FASCINATING AÏDA
SINGLE, I SAY
'GET KNOTTED'.
AND THEY
STORM OUT!

'. . . above all, thank you for not allowing yourselves to be manipulated by those whose artistic concern is nil.'

'Nil illegitimi carborundum.'

Our correspondents ranged in age from 17 to 85. Marilyn had the most fans, but Adèle and I had one admirer each so we were happy.

Many of the letters were very moving. One lady who told us that she was stuck at home with her two children, said that we reminded her of the sense of humour that she and her sister and her best friend shared, but her husband didn't understand.

Another lady who'd lost her fiancé in the Second World War and hadn't had much of a life since, said that it was the first time she'd felt she had something in common with the younger generation since her own youth. 'My sister and I . . . being two poor old fuddy-duddies who ride and windsurf wish you well from our retirement.'

We replied to them all – it was a monumental job, but so many of them had shared intimate details of their lives with us that each required a personal answer.

The documentary definitely altered our lives. Rachel, our agent, was bombarded with anxious calls from Arts Centres who'd previously been sniffy about booking us. And suddenly the audiences were friendlier: they came ready to laugh instead of sitting there bewildered for the first thirty minutes as they watched three daft overdressed women capering about.

There were two incidents that marked the change in our fortunes. Our first gig after the film was at the Donmar: it was a late night show and we broke the box office record. We'd just done a five week Christmas show there and hadn't exactly set the place on fire so we couldn't believe our ears when we were told of the huge queue at the box office. And when we came on, the audience cheered and cheered before we'd even sung a note.

The other incident happened at Cardiff. We'd been booked to do a Foyer Performance at St David's Hall, and on the day of the documentary we'd sold precisely four tickets. The day after, all 300 seats were sold out. The booker contacted Rachel, and asked if we'd agree to take the risk of going into the main concert hall (a 2,000 seater) instead as it happened to be empty that night.

'2,000 seats!' we squeaked in fear.

'Well, it's not quite as bad as it sounds,' said Rachel, 'because they'd curtain off the choir stalls behind the stage, and then it only holds 1,500 seats.'

It still didn't seem feasible that we could sell anything like 1,500 seats, but Rachel assured us that even as few as 600 people would make the place look fairly full so we agreed.

I have laughed more tonight than I can ... doing for years at anything on T.V. You have the ... engaging wit and sparkle, a wondrous mix of bawdiness ... sophistication. I wish you had recorded 'K.Y.' or 'Herpes' – ... maybe not so commercially successful but outstandingly funny and ... original, and, I think, very 'you'! Dear 'Fascinating Aida,

tell you how much I ... I had to write and ... minutes programme. My only complaint was ... too many 'Wally's' and not enough Sweet F.A.

Dear Fascinating Aida / You are bloody marvellous and ... make those BBC pansies look ... comedy act they are. (Actually, you ... to give them a bit of credit ... letting the show go out.)

I really would like to
have some of your stuff on tape, record or whatever, but I really don't want the
BBC production job - it kx makes you sound like, oh I don't know, 'dated' is
definitely the word. Isn't there any way you can produce some live stuff, that
hasn't been 'produced' to death?

A few days later, Rachel rang me.

'Dillie!' It was her turn to squeak. 'We've sold 721 seats!'

Two days later: 'We've sold 802 seats!'

Every day Rachel, who was as over-excited as we were, rang to find out how many tickets had gone. When we passed the 1,000 mark, we swooned.

We arrived there a few hours before the performance. Nearly 1,400 tickets had been sold, and we each had a dressing room with a bed *and* a shower. If we hadn't been so nervous it could have gone to our heads. And we did sell out – 1,534 tickets in all (shall we ever forget?) and the audience were rapturous. It was the most thrilling evening of our career to date.

The next day the local paper gave us a stinking review. That's showbiz for you.

'Get Knotted' gave us a bit of a fright by getting into the charts for three successive weeks. It went from No. 186, to No. 178, to No. 164. We were terrified it would keep on climbing as we'd look awful eejits if it was a hit after all the dreadful things we'd said about it. But thankfully, it then sank into the obscurity it deserved, and is now only played regularly on Radio Gibraltar.

CHAPTER ELEVEN

THE NET CLOSES IN

By Easter 1985, we were happily swinging into a three week season at the Lyric Theatre, Hammersmith. Bookings were piling up and everything was going swimmingly.

One day while we were rehearsing at Hammersmith, Jo, the publicity suprema, came up to Nica and me looking anxious and took us aside.

'I don't want to worry you,' she said, 'but I've had a couple of phone calls from the press. They're asking about Adèle, and I'm not quite sure what to say to them.' It transpired that two (or maybe more) journalists had got wind of Adèle's secret, and were trying to pressurise Jo into telling them the truth.

This was the start of several months of being hounded by hacks after a sensational story: 'WACKY GIRL TRIO IN SEX SECRET SCANDAL'. We were just about well known enough for that. Never mind how much Adèle had suffered, or that she was entitled to her privacy: the journalists grubbed around, sniffing, probing and threatening.

Nica and Rachel were rung up at regular intervals: 'Why don' you tell us the truth?' they'd ask. 'We know she's a sex change.'

Nica and Rachel denied it to the last. Then Adèle's parents were rung up, once by a man using a nickname for Adèle that she had never been called. The man claimed to be an old friend from University who had been abroad for many years (how convenient! and just wanted to look up his old friend while he was in th country, but as Adèle rightly said, no friend, close or otherwise from her Birmingham days would have ever used that particula nickname.

Another time her parents were rung up late one Friday night 'Give us a comment,' said the voice. 'We're going to print it o Sunday in the *News of the World* anyhow, so you might as well sa something.'

Adèle's old department at college was contacted. Would the please talk about their ex student? Or could they maybe suppl some photographs of her in her previous identity that might just b lying around in a drawer – some old production photos, pe haps . . . ?

A fellow student was traced to Scotland, where he had been livin for some time. Could he verify what the press knew to be the trut about Adèle? Or even give one comment: that would do just nicely

People we'd worked with on the cabaret circuit were contacte for information. Even Rory Bremner, who'd once had an innocent dinner with Adèle, was rung up out of the blue and asked to comment about his relationship with 'his girlfriend'. One dinner doesn't make a girlfriend. It would have been laughable if it hadn't been so distasteful. Marilyn and I felt completely trapped, and poor Adèle was distraught.

Things went from bad to worse. In May, we were overworked as usual: doing too many gigs and trying to record our album. Our collective nerves were fraying and what with the pressure of the press probes, none of us was very easy to live with.

Eventually, we had a stormy meeting. Nica, Rachel, Marilyn, and I had come to a group decision that we must release the story ourselves. We were damned if some seedy hack was going to make a couple of grand out of smearing Adèle's past all over the gutter press. The number of phone calls was mounting all the time and it was bound to come out in the end. We felt we should contact someone in the quality press and ask them to write an article revealing the truth in as non-salacious a manner as possible.

Adèle saw it differently. She was so hemmed in that she couldn't see the wood for the trees. I think she felt that if she hung on for ever, eventually 'they' would go away. We'd got to the stage where we weren't prepared to give her a choice any longer: we were willing to support her to the last, we told her, but if she wanted to be a star, as she had always told us, she would have to live with the consequences. We have always worked on majority rule and miserable though she was, she had to accept our decision. I know we made the right decision, though it was very nerve wracking at the time.

There was, of course, a selfish motive in our action. We, being nice middle-class girls, had never wanted to be scandalous and were horrified that we could, by association, be dragged into disrepute for the nation to relish: none of us liked the prospect of notoriety. We wanted our work to be liked and respected and the thought of having audiences who treated us as a freak show (which I feel they would have had we left the story to the predators) was horrendous. And it was unthinkable that we could let Adèle be treated as a freak. We'd known her for about 16 months, and not only had we long felt that she was right not to tell us originally, we never at any stage thought that she had made the wrong decision about what to do with her life.

It has been suggested that we knew Adèle's secret all along and simply used the story to get press attention. This makes me very angry, because nothing could be further from the truth. Had that been the case, we would neither have clammed up for so many months, nor would we have restricted the news to a discreet interview in the *Sunday Times*. And later when a notorious scandal sheet offered us a large sum of money for 'the story', we turned it down flat.

I sometimes try to imagine what it must be like to have all your most intimate secrets plastered over the newspapers. It must ruin many people's lives. My attitude to the press has been consistent; there are many good, honourable journalists who *are* trustworthy, and there are the ferrets who will stop at nothing in their pursuit of smutty stories to pander to the public's prurience on a Sunday.

I had confided Adèle's secret to quite a few journalists, not all of whom were personal friends. We were doing quite a number of articles for various organs. They were, naturally, asking questions about our childhoods, and I was anxious that they should not feel angry that Adèle had misled them about hers. Not one of them betrayed our trust.

We contacted my old friend Amanda Walker, who'd engineered that first gig on Capital Radio, and told her we wanted to release the story.

Amanda spent three days trying to contact the then editor of the *Guardian* women's page which we felt was the ideal place to break the story. We couldn't get past the secretary, who wouldn't under any circumstances put us through to the editor without more information, and we weren't willing to divulge any details to just anyone. It was curious that with Amanda's press credentials we got so little joy out of them.

The phone calls were getting more threatening and the story was developing into a race between journalists claiming to represent the *News of the World* and the *Mail on Sunday*. At length, Amanda rang a friend on the *Sunday Times* who put us in touch with Henry Porter who writes the People Page. Yes, he would cover the story: he hated the gutter press and was delighted to help us.

He came to meet us at the Donmar. Marilyn and I were extremely relieved. Adèle was tense, naturally, but Henry did an excellent interview and the story was published a week later.

And that was nearly that. Journalists would bring it up from time to time but we'd smile frostily and politely refuse to talk about it.

Some months later, after the 1985 Edinburgh Festival, the front page headline we'd dreaded appeared in the *Scottish Sunday Mail*.

'SEX SECRET OF FESTIVAL SMASH HIT!'

And who was the one who laughed most? Adèle. Well, they also described her as 'an attractive brunette tipped for stardom'.

A matter of identity

FASCINATING Aida is something to do with opera; it is a group of women dedicated to the rabid abuse of masculinity; it consists of three singers who were born to womanhood and desire separate development from men.

None of these statements is true. In fact, Fascinating Aida is simply a humorous and talented trio which has nothing to do with high opera and very little association with the feminist cause.

The surprising thing, particularly in view of the photograph on the left, is that they were not all born women. Adele Anderson, the newest member of the group, spent the first 20 or so years of her life as a man.

She underwent an operation to change her sex shortly after graduating from a drama course at Birmingham University. She disappeared into the civil service while the metamorphosis took place and spent some unproductive years working in job centres and the like.

While not a conventional step, this is by no means a novelty. Many who have felt ill at ease in their bodies have taken the same course. April Ashley was written about and Jan Morris wrote about it. You might reasonably think that quite enough has been said on the subject.

However, there is still considerable interest in the tabloid press, which is longing to reveal exclusively her story under a headline "Sex-op man in Libbers group". These stories are usually preceded by unwarranted intrusions into the subject's life.

Adele, aged 33, has put up with quite a bit of this recently. "Well, they telephoned all my friends, people I knew at university. They asked one person to send pictures of me before my operation. They telephoned my parents, pretending to be old friends from university, using a nickname which I never had and asking for my number."

All this has caused considerable upheaval in the group who have created a very individual career for themselves since last year's Edinburgh Festival. It is neither radical, popular in the strict sense, nor serious.

The group's other members, Dillie Keane and Marilyn Cutts, were anxious about the effect of exposure. This is understandable, as Adele did not tell them about her operation.

"Well, I had suspected for a while," said Dillie, "and I was a bit annoyed that she hadn't told us, but it is not blameworthy."

Adele defends her secrecy: "At first when I joined 18 months ago, I thought I was on a three-month trial and so I didn't tell them. Then when I was in the group, I didn't feel it was necessary because they had accepted me."

I divined a difficulty in the area of her secrecy. I do not think it would be exaggerating the situation to say that Marilyn and Dillie had formed a women's group and fully expected those who wanted to join to be women who've always been women.

Still, they seem to have got over this and one hopes that their genuine talent goes to achieve greater recognition.

The Henry Porter piece, 'A Matter of Identity', which appeared in the Sunday Times on 2nd June 1985.

Adèle's comments:

The story broke but, I'm happy to report, I did not. Strangely, it was a relief not to have to watch one's ps and qs any more. 'Yes, it's true,' we'd say politely, 'but it's not relevant. Now what shall we talk about?' As if by magic the phone calls ceased and my parents could once again enjoy an uninterrupted night's sleep. Audiences could stop cudgelling their brains about it, sit back and enjoy the show. Men could stop asking me out now they knew they'd get their names in the papers if they did.

I shouldn't complain. I got off lightly compared to other transsexuals who've been pursued by Fleet Street (or should we call it Wapping nowadays?) Tulah, the model who starred in a Smirnoff ad and a Bond movie, found herself out in the cold when the News of the World hit the streets with their exposé. In April 1986 Rachel Webb, a Labour Councillor in Lambeth, was vilified by a majority of the newspapers who delighted in revealing that she'd fathered several children. Yes, I was lucky and it's because I wasn't alone, I was a member of a group with a reputation for being able to stand up for themselves. (Let's face it: who'd cross swords with Dillie when her blood's up?) People liked what we did. As a spokesman for the Wogan Show said after being quizzed if the producers 'knew' about me: 'Fascinating Aïda were chosen to appear simply because they are a very talented act.'

And that's far more important to an audience than what I did ten years ago.

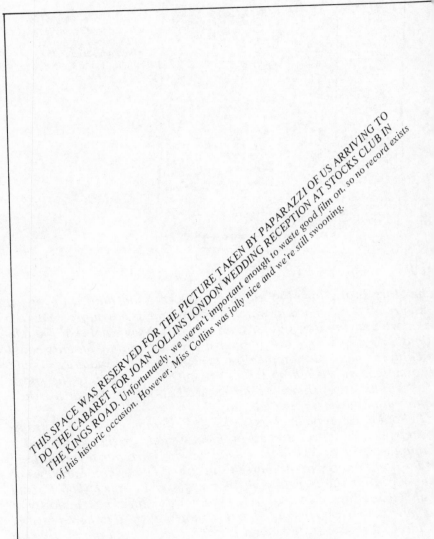

THIS SPACE WAS RESERVED FOR THE PICTURE TAKEN BY PAPARAZZI OF US ARRIVING TO DO THE CABARET FOR JOAN COLLINS LONDON WEDDING RECEPTION AT STOCKS CLUB IN THE KINGS ROAD. Unfortunately, we weren't important enough to waste good film on, so no record exists of this historic occasion. However, Miss Collins was jolly nice and we're still swooning.

ANOTHER MAN

I'd lived on my own for a while;
Developed a fine sense of style:
I knew all the answers —
Or thought I did —
Until something happened
Which blew off the lid:
I met a man, the sort of whom I'd always dreamed,
But the situation was not all it seemed:

I fell in love with a man in love with another man:
Didn't know it when we met up;
No-one told me of his set up;
How I wish I could have known before the whole affair began;
Didn't twig when he told me he shared a flat with Jake:
Boy, what a fool I was to make such a mistake
I fell in love with a man in love with another man.

Fell in love with a guy in love with another guy;
Thought that I'd spot one a mile off —
Well it surely wiped my smile off
When he told me very gently it wasn't even worth a try;
I felt sure I was the woman to change his mind;
But he said he wasn't the marrying kind,
I fell in love with a guy in love with another guy.

He offered me friendship — I mistook it for more:
Fancied he might want to share the rent;
I started making eyes
And didn't realise
When he asked me home for coffee that was all he meant:

Fell in love with a man . . .
And it seems so damn ironic
That our friendship is platonic
And the best that I can ever be is just an also ran.
Looking back I can't believe I could have been so crass,
They never taught us this in biology class —
Fell in love with a man in love . . .

I know I shouldn't blame myself or feel any shame;
'Cause next time round it'll be much the same;
I'll fall in love with a man in love with another dame.

Words: Adèle Anderson and Dillie Keane
Music: Dillie Keane
© 1985

CHAPTER TWELVE

GOODBYE DILLIE,
I MUST LEAVE YOU . . .

In November 1985, Marilyn decided she wanted to leave, and would do so after our forthcoming Australian tour so that we'd have plenty of time to find a replacement.

There were a number of reasons for this. We were by now on the road constantly: Adèle and I were happy as sandpersons as it gave us an excuse to have lunch at the Little Chef every single day, but Marilyn wasn't so enthusiastic. The more she watched us tucking gleefully into the Mushrooms in Breadcrumbs then an American Breakfast (with extra portion of Hash Browns, please) followed by Pancakes with Mapleen Syrup, the more she felt travel sick. In the end we never saw her because she was always tucked up and fast asleep on her little bed at the back of the van.

Her unhappiness began to show more and more. Regularly, she'd express a yearning to settle down and have some children, something I've never been that bothered about, and she realised that being continually on the move is a killer to romance.

It started to get awkward at interviews, because the question always came up: 'You look as though you're having a wonderful time up there on stage. Do you enjoy your job as much as you seem to?' A long, embarrassed silence would follow as Adèle and I hung our heads, waiting for Marilyn to say, 'No, I don't, actually. I'd rather be acting.' Marilyn is a painfully honest person, and we couldn't expect her to lie about it, but on the other hand it made us feel like berks.

Our personal relationship deteriorated. All our differences that had made us laugh for so long began to chafe. Like a marriage, it's the tiny things that have you reaching for the bread knife. I remember reading a Chekhov short story about a man who was driven to a frenzy by the sight of the little wispy hairs on the back of his wife's neck.

With Marilyn and me, it was probably dead pig and cottage cheese that broke the camel's back. I like delicious, crispy, smoked Irish bacon: plates and plates of it. She likes great tubfuls of tasteless, lumpy, disgusting white goo. (Who's prejudiced?)

When you're on the road, you're together for twenty-four relentless, remorseless hours a day. Tours stretch on indefinitely: one ends and another starts a few weeks later. Even when we're not touring, there's some sort of business that constantly demands our

attention: programmes to be recorded, songs to be written, letters to be answered, meetings to attend, new shows to devise . . . endless, endless work. There's no escaping from each other, and Marilyn felt more and more like an outsider. I don't know how it happened, and I'm dreadfully sorry that it did.

Marilyn's not one for aggressive assertiveness, unlike me who can make running into Genghis Khan feel like tea at the vicarage. She stays away from trouble when she can. Because she kept her head down and her trap shut, we knew less and less what she was thinking. So we'd ride roughshod over her feelings without knowing what her feelings were: e.g. we'd make decisions that she didn't like but didn't like to tell us she didn't like. The more this happened, the more she kept miserably silent, and the more we rode roughshod over her feelings. It was a vicious spiral.

So by the time Marilyn decided to leave, we all knew that it was for the best. She has been deluged with offers of acting work and rightly so, and we hope that she'll still come back to write with us from time to time.

People seemed to think it was the end of the world when they heard that Marilyn was leaving. Adèle and I tried not to be downcast, however. Working conditions had not been happy for some time. Fascinating Aïda is one of those groups that has thrived on changes. With this in mind we decided not even to attempt to get a straight replacement for Marilyn, and to try and see if we could find someone completely different, perhaps someone who wasn't white and middle class. The only prerogative was that her voice should be as good as Marilyn's and blend well with ours, because Marilyn had lots and lots of fans who would be very hard on someone with a less perfect voice.

So with high hopes we quickly placed an advertisement in *The Stage* (we had to act fast as we were off to Australia in a couple of months): 'Fascinating Aïda require actress/singer, soprano with range F to top B♭ : age thirty-ish-ish.' We were deluged with replies ranging from girls in gymslips to ladies who had passed their prime in 1930. (I mean, I know we're old, but . . .) We saw about eighty of these, and the search became more and more depressing.

It certainly made us realise how outstanding Marilyn's singing voice is. Lots of the girls had bags of talent, but there were very few who were on a par with Marilyn vocally, and if the voice *was* great, there was always some hitch. Either they were 4′ 11″ and made Adèle and I look like giantesses, or they took one look at us and thought better of signing their lives away for a couple of years to work with two people who were obviously dangerously mad. Some

Marilyn, looking like a young Ava Gardner, snapped by Tim O'Sullivan. (It's hardly surprising she's been inundated with job offers.)

Adèle and Dillie take the news of Marilyn leaving calmly. (Note the imaginative use of tights.)

interpreted the word 'singer' very liberally, and indeed I've had to revise my opinion on Nica's voice as a result: after hearing some auditionees sing I feel that Nica could hold her own in a one-woman tribute to Sondheim at the English National Opera with the Royal Philarmonic Orchestra.

There's a school of auditioning that thinks it advisable to go dressed for the part: on that basis we should be performing at the Windmill the way a couple of the girls turned up. I was always most impressed with those who turned up in neat, unfussy, working clothes, who sang short, well chosen and well presented songs, and who didn't arrive with illegible, handwritten music or songs that were too difficult to play.

It was disheartening to see so many people, especially those who'd been to one of the 'good' drama schools, showing that they had absolutely no audition technique. This is a major failing on the part of the drama schools: the students spend three years and a lot of money doing a very exhaustive, exhausting acting course and then are thrown out into the world without the slightest idea of how to sell themselves. We had people so covered in layers of clothes, hats, and scarves that you couldn't possibly gauge what they'd look like on stage in evening dress. We had girls come in having prepared an obscure nineteenth century bawdy house song, or whatever they'd chosen, and then they'd proceed to sing all eighteen verses. *Never* bore the auditioners should be rule number one.

No wonder we love our audiences, with correspondents like Angela Pink of Sydney.

Some people came in and apologised before they even sang a note: 'I'm sorry, I haven't sung this song in ages,' they'd say blithely. How do they expect anyone to employ them if they can't even put in a bit of work on their audition piece? I got irritated at this, and as for the ones who came in and said 'What's this audition for?' or 'What do you do?' It doesn't say much for you if you can't even be bothered to find out who or what you're auditioning for.

We saw quite a few North Americans, and every single one did an excellent audition. Selling oneself is part of the American Way of Life, and it sure would pay off for British actors to let a little of the American professionalism rub off on them. We were stunned when one girl turned up looking much prettier than her very unflattering photograph: Nica mentioned this, saying she didn't think the photo did our auditionee justice, and was told very sourly that she needn't be so patronising. Nica was only trying to be professionally encouraging.

It may seem as if I'm telling tales out of school by talking so disparagingly of some of the people who came to find a job with us. But we've all been on the other side: we remembered only too clearly how painful the audition process is and we genuinely wanted each and every person who auditioned for us to be excellent. I would have been very grateful for any help at all, so if anyone does gain something from what I've written, then I'll have done some good after all.

Dillie's Bitter Experience Audition Tips

Pre-audition selling technique

1.   *Photograph:* one 5″ × 7″ (or 10″ × 8″ if you're feeling
      rich) close up of your head and shoulders: don't send lots o
      shots of you in character as Widow Twanky or Burlingto
      Bertie: they're a waste of money and give much les
      information than a good, clear head shot. It also must look
      like you – not like you'd like to look. If you send in a snap
      of yourself looking like Greta Garbo and turn up looking
      like Minnie Mouse, then the chances are you won't get the
      job.

2.   *The C.V.:* Send in a clearly typed curriculum vitae, with
      proper margins and headings so that the salient facts are
      easy to pick out immediately. Don't make it *too* detailed bu
      give the important facts of your life. Don't be deliberately
      misleading (e.g. don't say you've played Portia at Stratford
      upon-Avon when what you actually did was tour *The*
      Merchant of Venice with a schools group and play at a
      comprehensive in Stratford one Wednesday last March). It'
      not worth lying: you'll be found out, and that makes people
      very angry. Don't exaggerate your capabilities either. A
      friend of mine said she could ride a horse; she got a job or
      the strength of it, and on the first day was thrown from the
      saddle, broke her ankle and lost the job.

3.   *S.A.E.:* If you want your photo back, don't enclose an s.a.e
      that's a quarter the size of your photograph. Enclose one o
      the proper size. Theatres are underfunded and understaffed
      time is short and it costs a surprising amount to send your
      photo back.

4.   *Preparation*: Try and find out what you're auditioning for. I
      it's for the part of a nineteenth century princess, it doesn'
      advance your cause to turn up in torn jeans and a leather
      jacket. Conversely, if the part is for a 1920s chorus girl
      there's no need to go the whole hog and dress the part
      completely. As a general rule directors have no imagination
      but don't like to admit it to themselves. If you do all the
      work for them, then they can't think that they've made a
      quantum leap by casting you. Therefore, when you're
      auditioning for the part of a 1920s chorus girl, you can go
      some way towards approximating the right look, but it's no

necessary to walk in looking a total anachronism. If you can't find out much about the job, or you're being auditioned for a variety of parts, wear something quietly flattering but not overdramatic: I was most interested in the girls who came in dressed in one colour track suits: they looked attractive, workmanlike and cheerful, and their clothes weren't distracting.

5.   *Hair*: On my knees, I beg you: comb your hair out of your eyes. The eyes are the window of the soul, and it's bloody silly to think that your long fringe which has them swooning in 'Snippers' is going to have the same effect at the audition. If you can't see the eyes, you can't see the face.

6.   *Feet*: If you think there's the remotest possibility that you might be asked to do some dancing, *don't* wear boots. Boots aren't a great idea anyhow because they restrict your movement much more than you think, unless they're those little button boots from Anello's which are made for dancing in.

7.   *Rehearsal*: If you can't be bothered to rehearse your audition piece, don't bother to go.

At the audition

8.   *Your entry*: Don't come in loaded up with coats, bags, cardys, etc. If you have to go to the audition with all your dance paraphernalia and your overnight bag, see if you can leave it outside the audition room. If you have to spend 60 seconds divesting yourself of all your winter wear, they'll be the longest 60 seconds you've ever spent. And if you've done a lousy audition and have to spend another minute putting it all on again in front of the tired auditioners, worse still. They've got to sit there with frozen smiles on their faces while you dress for a stroll in Siberia. So come in without your coat, simply dressed, and with, if possible, just the one bag.

9.   *First impression*: Come in quickly, put your bag down, and say, 'Hello, I'm Meryl Peters' or whatever your name is. Sit if you're asked to: otherwise remain standing. For heaven's sake, *smile*. It really does help if you appear likeable: nobody wants to work with a sourpuss.

10.   *Singing*:

    (a)   If you've been asked to bring a song, have the music ready, and don't spend hours scrabbling at the bottom of your knapsack for it.

    (b)   Don't bring an illegible handwritten song from that one woman musical of yours: 'Mrs. Beeton, the Politics of Cooking' may have been a smash at the York and Albany but it also may be incomprehensible in the context of an audition.

    (c)   Don't bring a song that needs transposing: if you must sing that song in another key, pay a music copyist to write out a neat, legible version in the key you want.

    (d)   Do make sure the song is in your range. If it has a top B ♭ that you can't reach, think about changing the song rather than muff the note. You can, of course, go for a lower note, but you may be spoiling the climax of the song.

    (e)   Choose a song that is easy to play and enjoyable to listen to. Plunder lesser known musicals and beware of Sondheim: he's very difficult to play and the songs seem deceptively easy to the singer.

    (f)   If you know you can't sing all that well, don't fall into the trap of thinking you can sing Kurt Weill. There are too many frog-voiced actresses around who think that if Lottie Lenya got away with it, they can. Remember Lottie Lenya was not only Weill's wife, but she was also intensely musical and though she had an odd, low voice, she sang the songs perfectly because he wrote them for her.

    (g)   If you've decided to sing 'Cabaret' or 'Don't Cry For Me, Argentina' or some other song that's immediately identified with a particular singer, think again: you've got to be very sure you can bring something new to the song, because it's very difficult for the listener not to compare you unfavourably with the original artiste.

    (h)   Try to choose a song that is not too far away from what you're auditioning for, i.e. avoid singing an American mining song if you're auditioning for *The Boyfriend*.

    (i)   Make sure the song suits your personality: if you're six foot six and built like a stevedore, think twice before you sing 'Jesus wants me for a sunbeam'. You may create a comic effect you had not intended.

    (j)   Understand what you're singing. There is a story about a girl who went for an audition and sang a song made famous by Rogers and Astaire. 'You say potay-to, and I say potay-to,' she sang; 'you say tomah-to, and I say tomah-to: potay-to, potay-to, tomah-to, tomah-to, let's call the whole thing off.' The director was so hysterical that he recalled her simply so that he could invite his friends in to see this girl who'd so hopelessly missed the point of the song.

(k) If an accompanist is provided, it's better not to sing unaccompanied: you're not giving a clear idea of your overall musicianship.

(l) Make your song *short*: one verse and one chorus is quite enough.

(m) If your auditioners say 'Thank you' at the end of a section, stop: don't plough on with the next seventeen choruses, thinking that because you've rehearsed them, you're damn well going to do them. Your auditioners have usually heard what they need in the first 90 seconds, and they won't feel very warm towards you if you waste their time.

(n) Don't grip the piano, or sing at the floor. Pick a space that's well lit if you're on a stage, and face the auditioners, not the corner. Look at them occasionally: don't stare them out, but don't avoid their gaze altogether. *Smile!*

(o) If you forget the words, don't fret. Stop, collect yourself, and go back to the beginning. Everyone forgets their lines from time to time.

11. *Audition piece*: The above applies to an audition speech as well as to a song. Make it snappy, and make sure it suits you.

12. *After the song*: When you've done your bits, don't settle in for a long cosy chat unless the auditioners obviously want to know more about you. Say thank you, and vamoose with *all* your belongings: it's embarrassing for you if you have to come back to collect your Sainsbury's bag.

13. *Questions*: Don't worry if you can't think of any intelligent questions to ask about the job. You don't have to be a Phi Beta Kappa to get the part.

After the audition . . .

14. Don't ring up every day to find out if you've got the part. You'll hear when they've made the choice, and it may take

quite a while for them to make up their minds. If you feel
you've got a reasonable chance, get your agent (if you have
one) to ring a few days later and make an enquiry.

I hope this helps someone.

Of the women we saw who were good, and there were quite a few
outstandingly talented women, only one had a voice that blended
with Adèle and me. We've got unusual voices, to say the least, and
the fact that Marilyn's glorious tones blended so superbly with our
throaty growls is a tribute to her musicianship rather than our
singing ability. Adèle could sing her harmonies with her head in a
cup of custard, as Pattie says, but I go out of tune immediately if I'm
singing with someone who's not quite in pitch herself.

The one who had all the attributes we were looking for was called
Sheila Brand: a tall, glamorous Canadian somewhere between a
Raymond Chandler and a Cole Porter type. However, she had
another attribute that we weren't looking for. When she auditioned,
she came in looking stunning, took off her voluminous coat and
underneath she was eight months pregnant. We overlooked the
bulge, I'm glad to say, and offered her the job, and she agreed to
think about it while we were down under.

So we went off to Australia not at all sure of our future.

*Denise, seated, with her pal Alex,
unaware that she is doing an
audition. (Snapped at the very party
where we first heard her sing.)*

*Julianne White, the World's Best
Tour Manager, snapped while we
were all trying not to blub during
our farewell at Perth Airport.*

*Dame Adèle Anderson —
Exploreuse. 'Jungle Holds*

Australia . . . Australia . . . Australia was everything and more we'd ever dreamed of. We went to Sydney, Alice Springs, Townsville, Perth, Geraldton, Karratha and Albany, and if I hadn't got so much to stay here for, i.e. work, boyfriend and family, I'd emigrate tomorrow. The people are open and generous to a fault: the country is spectacularly beautiful and the sun shines all the time. The show went down better than we could ever have imagined, and we're hoping to go back there next year: well, we've got to – Nica and Adèle both fell in love. So did I, but with Australia, not any one person in particular.

While we were in Sydney, something momentous happened: we went to a party.

We'd been semi-adopted by a couple who we met on the first night: a Scotsman called Michael Haeburn-Little who was now living in Australia, and was on the Sydney Festival Committee. After our show, he introduced himself and asked Adèle and me if we'd like to go out drinking with him and a few pals. We needed no encouragement, and ended up getting tight as corsets till five in the morning with him and his girlfriend, a singer/actress called Denise Wharmby. One thing led to another, and we met up with them pretty regularly for late night drinking sessions.

They decided to throw a barbecue for us one Sunday. We had a great day lolling in their garden being wined and dined, and were just about to leave to go out to another dinner in the evening when someone asked Denise to sing.

'Let's just stay and hear one song,' I said to the others, pleadingly. They rolled their eyes heavenwards, thinking that they'd never get me away once the sing-song started, and put their handbags down.

Denise sang two duets with a friend of hers: 'I Know Him So Well' from *Chess* and a classical duet. They both had excellent voices but Denise's was quite remarkable: besides which Denise played the piano for one of the songs and played almost as well as she sang.

Then Alex, the other girl, said 'Sing "Sempre Libera", Denise.' (It's the monstrously difficult aria from *La Traviata*.)

'Oh, gee . . . I haven't sung it for six months,' said Denise: '. . . well, all right.' (This was a party, not an audition!)

The only way I can describe the next few minutes is to say that it was one of those rare moments when you're granted a glimpse of heaven. In a tiny drawing room in Sydney where there was barely room for anything other than the grand piano, I heard one of the world's greatest arias sung perfectly when all I had been expecting was a nice afternoon at a barbecue. Those notes . . . that voice . . . the incredible brilliance and faultless technique . . . The hairs on the back of my neck were nearly plaiting themselves and by the end I

Sequins are out of the question in the heat of the noonday sun at Alice Springs.

Back in London, Dillie and Adèle out with Rachel who is preparing to welcome our new Australian member by getting into typical Antipodean clothing. Nica points out that Rachel has been several hours in the preparation and looks every bit as Australian as an Arbroath Smokie.

had tears pouring down my cheeks – I felt like a complete berk.

Then we had to go as we were getting late, and I sat in the car with Nica and Adèle babbling incoherently about Denise.

'We've *got* to audition her for the group,' I said manically. 'If Sheila turns us down, we need to have someone else in mind.'

'Don't be impractical, Dillie,' said Nica. 'Yes, of course she's wonderful, but we'll never get a work permit for her.'

I wouldn't let up, though, and a few days later we auditioned her. She sang every bit as well as before, and revealed not only that she played the piano, but that she juggled and could play the violin while standing on one leg on a tightrope. She seemed to be enthusiastic about joining, so we were honest with her and told her it was a long shot as (a) we'd already offered the job to someone who we thought was ideal, and (b) even if Sheila turned us down, we had to give preference to a British citizen. Still, we told her that we thought she was outstanding and would keep her very much in mind. For my own part, to have a voice like that in the group would be a great inspiration.

We trailed back to wintry old Britain, and shortly after Sheila told us that she had, after all, decided it was too much of an undertaking to join FA with a new baby in tow. So we started auditioning again, and it was the same story as before. Plenty of talent, but nobody that blended.

So to my great joy we've decided on Denise, and she'll have joined us by the time this is published. We'll take the immigration problems as they come: we think we'll at least get a six month work permit and after that we'll keep everything crossed.

Denise Wharmby — the new member

P.S. from Denise (Yes, I finally arrived!)

... My friends back home were extremely pleased when I told them they would be seeing the last of me for a while. I was bombarded with enthusiastic questions about 'Fascinating Aïda', not many of which I could answer adequately, so I can now send them copies of this book and let them read for themselves. I've been designated this page to outline my career to date, and all that led up to my joining F.A.

I began my musical training at the age of seven, and actually toured England and Wales in 1971 with the Rosny Children's Choir, performing at the Welsh International Eisteddfodd, Westminster Abbey and other monumental places. We were an instant hit, and my endless appetite for travel was firmly established from that moment onwards. I finished my conservatorium course in classical piano and singing, and ventured from the very friendly but culturally stultifying shores of Tasmania to Melbourne in 1978. Broadcasts, recitals for the BBC and competitions followed, as a concert pianist. All seemed like endless hard slog with not much remuneration, so I auditioned for Barnum, *the circus musical, initiating four years of almost non-stop work as a singer. I was employed as understudy to Charity Barnum and opera singer Jenny Lind, then took over the role of Jenny Lind towards the end of the run. During the show, I acquired numerous skills such as juggling, tightrope-walking and trapeze. A national tour of* Jesus Christ, Superstar *followed, then I was asked to play the part of Edith in* The Pirates of Penzance. *(Could this be fate entwining Dillie Keane and myself?)* Pirates *gave me work for three extremely successful seasons (it smashed all box office records in Australia) and in between re-runs, the gaps were filled with multifarious engagements, including* Side By Side By Sondheim, Kiss Me Kate, They're Playing Our Song *as principal pianist, and as Musical Director of children's musicals.*

Of the party in Sydney, which had become my home, all I can say is that I was certainly in the right place at the right time. My advice to any hopefuls in this business: let your natural talent shine through as I did (after 10 glasses of gin).

I now look forward to an exciting and action-packed time with Fascinating Aïda. *Many thanks to Dillie, Adèle and Nica for choosing me.*

CHAPTER THIRTEEN

ALL THOSE QUESTIONS
ANSWERED ONCE AND FOR ALL

1.   *How did you get your name?*
      See Chapter Five.

2.   *Is it true, Adèle?*
      See Chapter Nine.

3.   *Do you write all your own songs?*
      No, Noel Coward comes to us in the night.

4.   *Will you sing my songs?*
      Yes, if you pay us £1,000,000.

5.   *Do you all live together?*
      Yes. Twenty-four hours a day isn't enough.

7.   *Are you really drunk on stage, Dillie?*
      No, I fall down all the time.

8.   *When did you leave Canada, Adèle?*
      That was Lizzie.

9.   *Why do you wear such outrageous dresses?*
      Because we're damned if Danny La Rue is going to get all
      the best frocks.

10.   *How tall are you really, Adèle?*
      5′ 9¾″, but I'm 6′ 4″ on stage.

11.   *Are you a natural blonde, Dillie?*
      Yes, and I'm 21.

12.   *How old are you all?*
      50, and we look wonderful for our age.

13.   *How did you like Australia?*
      Our emigration papers are being processed at the
      moment.

14.   *What does your mother think of the act, Dillie?*
      Next question?

15.   *Why aren't you feminists?*
      Who says we aren't?

16.   *Are you still driving around in that old van?*
       Yes, we love breaking down every few miles: it makes the
       tour so much more thrilling.

17.   *Are you really all Sloane Rangers?*
       Boring, boring, very very boring, okay, ya?

18.   *How do you learn all those lines?*
       Nica whips us till we remember them.

19.   *Why do you work with a director?*
       We need a referee.

20.   *Why have there been so many changes of personnel?*
       Because Dillie's impossible to work with.

21.   *What do you think you'll all be doing in ten years time?*
       Giving way to the younger generation.

22.   *What are you doing now?*
       Giving way to the younger generation.

23.   *Why don't you sing any Andrews Sisters songs?*
       'Cause we write our own, schmuck chops.

24.   *How would you describe yourselves?*
       Oh, help . . .

25.   *Do you have a heroine?*
       Yes, Nica Burns. She puts up with so much.

26. *Why did you write this book?*
    Vast egos and a fat cheque.

27. *What on earth do you do during the day?*
    Loll about drinking champagne with handsome princes,
    and everything magically gets done.

28. *How do you stay so slim?*
    Stay up all night and drink loads of black coffee.

29. *Do you feel you represent young women of today?*
    Where's the exit?

30. *Why Malcolm and Gordon?*
    They were my best buddies at drama school.

MALCOLM

GORDON

31. *Fascinating Who?*
    Aaaarrrghhhh . . . .

JEALOUSY

Jealousy — my jealousy
Keeps tearing at my soul:
Jealousy — tormenting me
So I just lose control:
Jealousy inflames my heart
But turns your love so cold.

Jealousy obsesses me
And ev'ry day I find
I can't get free from this misery
Of love and hate entwined:
Since we met I haven't had
A moment's peace of mind.

And all the time the days and nights get longer:
Don't know myself any more.
My twisted passion always growing stronger:
I drive away the one I adore:

Haunting me and taunting me,
Suspicion's here to stay:
I can't believe you won't deceive
No matter what you say.
The more my hunger for you shows
The more you turn away.

Don't need a reason to feel the way I do:
I lose my reason ev'ry time I look at you.

I see you lock'd in all those hot embraces
With girls you loved before we met.
I conjure up a hundred thousand faces
Of all the women you don't even know yet.

Jealousy — my jealousy
Keeps tearing at my soul:
Jealousy — tormenting me
So I just lose control:
Jealousy inflames my heart
But turns your love so cold.

Don't need a reason to feel the way I do:
I lose my reason ev'ry time I look at you.

My jealousy
Sweet jealousy
Jealousy.

Words: Adèle Anderson and Dillie Keane
Music: Dillie Keane
© 1985

CHAPTER FOURTEEN

THE BRONTËS

or

OUR ALTER EGOS

Hi! Hi evvybody! This is Emmy-Lee speakin, as per usual. I always do the speakin fer me n mah sisters on account of they bein busy with difrent hobies. My FAVRIT sister Charlotte is nachrally bein wind and dind by some oil millionare er uther, and muh other sister Anne is heah beside me but she's chained to the chair so she cain't go anywhere unsavry, lahk a bar frinstance.

Now lots of you wunnerful folks've bin writin ter me, askin fer a little run-down on our persnal histry, so as Fascinatin Angela couldn't think of anything to fill these pertikler pages, we thought we'd use the oppertunity ter speak to y'all. They offen come on tour with us as support act and I kin tell you they mosly ain't got nuthin passin through their heads.

So here goes. I'm gwine ter tell you a little ol bit bout our background.

We was born, few years ago now, out of the head of Millie Kane, who plays pianny with Fascinatin Tosca, jes lahk that goddess who burst from the head of some god er other. Jehupiter, or somebody lahk that. That was a purty appropriate way ter be born, cause many people think we are goddesses — well, me 'n' Charlotte heah.

This girl (girl, huh! she's forty if she's a day!) Lilly

Kearns, she'd bin to see a certin gintleman called Hank Wangford who's a Country and Western starlet upon these shores, and so much was she struck bah this gintleman's antics upon the stage that Billy wint home with her brain so full of idees it was almos fit ter burst.

Nex mornin, Gilly woke up and suddenly we popt into her mind: we'd been out there in the ether waitin fer the right brain to pop into for years and years, 'n' whin the right one kept not comin along, we popt into hers instead. Which is why we turned out jes a little bit wonky: leastways, Charlotte 'n' I turned out jes fine but Anne ain't so well in her mind. We gotta look after her all the time cause she jes drinks licker all the time and costs us a fortune in hospittle fees, n she's bin to the Betty Ford Clinic more times n I care to re-call.

Well, we wus born jes lahk that, grown-up 'n' evvything, with three seprit personalities, 'n' named after those original Queens of Country, the Fabulous Brontë Sisters. (Cept we're American.) I so admire their work: I've bought all their books. We got a brother too called Branston, but he's even worse'n Anne, he's pickled all the tahm, so we don' see too much o' him if we kin help it. He's a part time mortuary beautician by trade, and often helps Anne with her make-up 'n' wigs. (She's got no hair at all — ain't that sad?)

I'm the elder of the three, so I'm the head o' the family, since Branston abregated his responsibilitys twards us. I look after passports 'n' such lahk, n collect Anne from lost propty departmints bout once in evvy week.

Muh favrit hobby is sightseein. I bin sightseein all ovuh the world, I seen the Tower of London, the

Mah sisters and mahself — mah favrit sister Charlotte lookin jes gorjus as evah and mah other sister Anne lookin as good as we could make her. As you will see, mah teeth wer very expinsiv.

Sister Anne livin' out the Betty Ford Precept: jog around the bar, not into it. That's me in the last picher — I had been tryin to perswede the bartender to a purer way o life.

Leanin' Tower of Eiffel, the Tower of Pizza, I jes' lerve towers. Cain't have enugh of them. I seen the Plutonium in Brussles, which is a building entirly made up of great big balls. I niver seen anything quite so pickulier. But ain't that the fun o' travellin, all those pickulier lil habits that forrign people got 'n' that we don have at home cause we're American?

I also bin to Australia whur I visited all over the place in Sidney mosly, meeting all the Sydwegians and goin to see the lil ol harber and their very own Grand Ol' Opry House. My, if anything's a pickulier bilding, that is, but then it takes all sorts, as my lil ol Maw always said.

We also visitid the Yulara National Park. Yulara, as you will know, is an Aboriginal word meaning Place Of No Surf. Whin we were there, we was

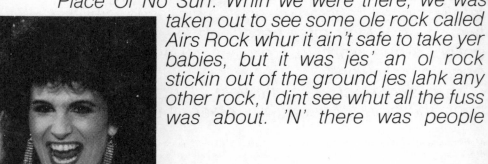

taken out to see some ole rock called Airs Rock whur it ain't safe to take yer babies, but it was jes' an ol rock stickin out of the ground jes lahk any other rock, I dint see whut all the fuss was about. 'N' there was people

climbing *up it, 'n' the big handsome ranger said did I want to climb up it 'n' I said why certainly not, I got my best high heels on. So I went back to the Sheriton Hotel and marveld at that instid.*

Course I don need ter tell you that muh FAVRIT sister Charlotte was perposed to all over Australia. Those hormoans o hers just hev men layin themselves down at her purty lil feet. She coulda had any number o bilyonairs marchin up the isle but she wus mornin for a lost love at the time, an besides she was haglin fer alimoney from one of her unberried exhusbands (mos of her husband hev been gatherd unto the boozum of Abriham) and she couldn accept any perposals fer fear of jepardizin her clame.

Nachrally sister Anne got inter all sorts o trouble in Australia; she said she dint care two pins if she saw the sun setting over any ole rocks, she jes wanned to wrap her lips around a stubby. Mos of the stubbies ran away from her tho, once they saw her dermatitis.

But you kin see that I'm a real serius sightseer, 'n' evvy time we go to a new town to bring our

*wunnerful tunes to poor folks who've saved up ɑ
their pennies fur munths ter see us, I go roun ɑ
the local sightseein spots so that I kin tell evvy boc
whin I'm on stage 'bout all the places I visited.
pleases folks iffen yer take an innerest in the
locale.*

*Charlotte ain't so innerested in sightseein as
am. She's bin married more times than I kin cour
She also suffers terribly from PMT so we have ⱼ
be gintle with her. Charlotte is always lookin' fer
father figger. Each n evvy one of her husbanc
ceptin Jim was very, very old, and mostly die
leavin her considrable sums of money. Jim wɑ
more lahk a brother figger, he was Sidney's be
friend since poor old Sid was a child at his mother
knee, and as you will know, Sid was Charlotte
affianced till he met a tragic death under the whee
of a passin lorry.*

*Jim dint last long in the hot seat – he '
Charlotte divorced a coupla months later. I figgere
she jes' married him fer comfort, he was sech
comfort to her when Sidney died untimely befoɾ
she was even eligible fer an
alimoney, and besides, sƕ
had the weddin' cake mad·
'n' a dress 'n' evvything, so
seemed a shame to let it ɡ
ter waste. An I jes lerѵ*

bein a bridesmade, so I hev ter admit I did a lil bit of in-courajment.

Yep, Charlotte was real broke up bout the whole affair, Sid goin and dyin lahk that on her, mos inconsidrit as usual, but Jim nobley stept into the breech and comforted poor sister Charlotte. Jim, of course, had bin steppin out with mah other sister, Anne, and there was talk of them gettin wed, but when Charlotte experted her considrable charms upon him, he was a goner. Anne dint seem to take it too hard, cept she's bin drunk evah since, so I reckin as how Jim was lucky to git outa that one and marry mah FAVRIT sister Charlotte instead, even if it was only for a very short time. Then whin he dint git that premotion he tol Charlotte he was gittin, she rightly felt lit down and gave him his marchin papers.

Then Jim tried to step out again with Anne, but she was so far gawn in sin and de-bauchery by that time that she tole him he could go 'n' boil his head, and a lot of other mighty uncivil things which I cannot repeat heah on account of bein a Baptist. She's only jealous of Charlotte who had more persnal charms where Jim was concernd. Charlotte has more o whats called feramoans than mos peple ever see in their lives.

Charlottes name has even bin linkt with Royalty but that jes came ter nothin cause they dint want another abdicatin situation, Charlotte bein pre-viously married so many times. So her prince and she were sundered jes lahk the story of the studint prince which Mario Lanza sung so heart breakinly (if you lahk that kinder music which persnly I don' it not bein Country and Western which is the only music werth lisnin to.)

Mah favrit sister Charlotte relivin the horable expereyunce of seeing Sid slither neath a great big truck to meet his Maker before he was expektin to, as she sings the painful baladd 'Sid'.

So the prince must go to his thrown without her, a brokin man. Course people think he's gwine ter be happy with Fergy, (aint that a pickulier name fer a girl?) but we all knows he's jes hidin' his pain for Charlotte. An' evvy single night, Charlotte kisses his picher which she keeps by her bed in her luxury trailer 'n' whispers, 'Nighty night, Drew darlin'!'

Well, that jes' leaves Anne, and I giss I better leave Anne too. She's jes sech a persnal libility. But thin, she has not bin visitid. Mah FAVRIT sister and I have bin visited by God many, many times, 'n' we have bin blest with many great 'n' wunnerful things, (I have good helth, strong teeth n an upright boozum) but Anne has NOT bin visitid. She has refused to see the light that shines on eachan evvy one of us. She jes spinds all o her time in bars, evah since Jim married Charlotte she gone right off the rails jes to spite her sister.

But thin, there has bin a considrable amount of persnal antaganism between those two evah since they was in dipers. Sister Anne had notions o bein a concert pianny player, but she'd bin having lessons for bout six months or so and still hadn't got any ferther than some fellers called Batoven and List who made her play horable ol fashiond music: rattle rattle rattle it wint! We could NOT listn with any pleashur, I kin tell you. Day in, day out, we heard a pathetic sonata, a shoppin symphony fer pianny, n sumthin else she calld 'My Zerkas'. Thos ol Zerkas gave us a pain in our ears, I kin tell you.

So Maw decided she had to stop her lecons, well she weren't gitting any better, jes noisier, n she refused ter play any of the sweet tunes we was brought up with, so mah FAVRIT sister Charlotte had lecons instid. She dint manage to git eny ferther than playin hang down yer hed, tom dooly, with one finger, but we likd it bitter than all that stuff Anne likd. Mah paw he used ter say that it was cobblers cos it was by Shoe Bert n Shoe Man but we dint unnerstand.

Still I spose Anns pianny trainin has come in usful as she plays fer us nowadays; its a kindness to giv sech a brokin soul imployment. Ceptin it has its libilties on account of her arms bein so punchered with holes that sometime she cant play too well.

Nevah mind, says my FAVRIT sister Charlotte, its cheaper n a band.

Well that's about all there is ter say bout us, I gotta hurry out 'n' do some sight seein in dear ol London town — how I do love it! Oh yes. It's so beautifly laid out. Dont know when it died, but its beautifly laid out.

Oh dear, while I bin writin this mah sister Anne seems to hev disappeard, she must have secreted a file about her person and sawd through the chain. I spex I'm gonna be bailin her outa some plice cell tmorrow mornin. Long as the plicemen are good lookin, I don mind!

Meanwhile, much love to all our fans, all you wunnerful folks out there keeping us in riches and gorgeous gowns. Jes keep buyin tickets woncher? Bah fer now, God bless, an remember the lil ol sayin, the cream of today is the cheese of tomorrer. Its stood me in good sted all these years and I'm perfickly sure itll help you folks. Bah!

GOD IS A TEXAN

(Spoken)

People go through life forever searchin'
Lookin' fer answers in the sky
And though it makes me grieve
There are those who don't believe
And what's more, they don' even try:
Now in Texas, we folks are mighty lucky
We got oil, we got money, we got land:
We got lots of sun and space:
We are God's chosen race,
And we're gwine ter reach the Promised Land . . .
Cause . . .

(Sung)

God is a Texan
God is a Texan
Ain't that vexin' for you?
He ain't a Turkish Dog
And he couldn't be a Frog,
He flies the flag that is red white and blue.
He flies the flag that is red white and blue.

Now God's on the side of the big battalions,
And we're the biggest and the best:
We'll rule the earth, the ocean blue,
The skies and the heavens too
To defend democracy in the West.
And we've got Ronnie to protect us from disaster,
From the enemies who threaten ev'ry day;
He's not a Texan, it is true,
But he's a cowboy — that'll do,
And he'll lead us the American Way.

Cause
God is a Texan
God is a Texan
And that is perplexin', I knows:
He ain't a pinko Commie
And he couldn't be a Pommie
He's under the yellow Rose.
He's under the yellow Rose.

God is a Texan
God is a Texan
He ain't a goddam Mex an' that for sure
You don' ketch him eatin Pasta
And please God he ain't a Rasta
And that's what keeps us pure.
And that's what keeps us pure.

God is a Texan
God is a Texan
And He'll keep his muscles flexin' fer thee
He is neither red nor yeller
He's a regular feller,
He's the one who'll keep us free.
He's the one who'll keep us free.

Words and Music: Dillie Keane
© 1985

Our FAVᴼRIT song!

CHAPTER FIFTEEN

GOODBYE AND GO

A friend of Adèle's went into the HMV shop some time ago to buy our single. Poor sap, you may say, and you'd be right, but each to his own, and who am I to cast aspersions on someone's musical taste when I admit to Arthur Sullivan being my favourite composer?

Anyhow, the said friend approached one of the vendors with a ready smile and a ready ready or two, and said brightly, 'Excuse me, have you got the single "Get Knotted" please?'

'Wha'?' replied the unusually charmless assistant. (I usually have better luck in HMV.) The question was repeated. ''Oo's it by?' he asked.

'It's by Fascinating Aïda,' said our man.

'Oh, you mean that feminist group!' sneered the assistant, and thus enlightened he snaked off reluctantly to get the record. Presumably he thought that being a feminist was tantamount to social hari-kiri. Perhaps feminists don't buy records.

Another story. My mother, a true blue in whom the spirit of Disraeli lives on undaunted, thinks we're suspiciously left-wing because we sing an angry song about unemployment. On the other hand, my sister, who is a block off the old chip, felt that our song about a mother and baby being imprisoned by fallout in a nuclear shelter could be taken as pro-Cruise. Curious, that.

Yet more views of FA. The *Mail on Sunday* hack who interviewed us, despite being repeatedly told that we hailed from such unspeakably non-U spots as Brixton, Portsmouth and Taunton, dubbed us Sloane Rangers in print. This would surprise my ex-school mates who are Range Rovers amongst Sloanes and probably consider my disdain for a life of Huskies and Hermes a hideous genetic error that my family have had to live down at all costs.

We've been called the Alternative Andrews Sisters, a female version of the Bonzo Dog Doo Dah Band, the female successors to Flanders and Swann, Noel Coward and Tom Lehrer and even a younger Hinge and Bracket. That, I'm sure you'll agree, is quite a range.

The point I'm trying to make in my circuitous way is that if people decide to view you in a certain light, there's damn all you can do to change their minds. They have a great need to pigeonhole you in their own special way before they can begin to understand you. I try not to mind being categorised in this way, except for that one occasion when it made us all extremely cross to be described as Sloane Rangers. However, we've recovered now, and at least we

Three not-so-wise monkeys — we'll have to get new photos now.

know that there's not a lot worse they can say about us.

As *City Limits* said, 'Biting? Well, it depends on where you're standing.' Exactly. The lady who wrote the outraged letter to us after our documentary seems to feel we're the natural successors to Xaviera Hollander. Others think us steamingly tame.

Looking at us from the inside, our attitude is that we're entertainers first and foremost, and not teachers. People pay their money to be entertained and it's a job in which I take a great deal of pride and pleasure. However, that alone isn't quite enough. We are actually our own worst critics and constantly revise and rework in the hope of improvement. We are scrupulously careful politically and morally, but we are not primarily a political group and nor do we want to be. We are all softly left wing and the shows always contain some indication of this – whether it be our song 'Bunker Lullaby' or another about unemployment, because we are all angry about unemployment and nuclear armament. But though these songs are what make the shows worthwhile for us, were we to harp on these themes for any longer than we do, it would make the show very turgid and dull. And when you have three (or rather, four, for I should include Nica) very strong personalities contributing their piece, and each with their separate pet moral or hobby horse, the end product inevitably runs the risk of being watered down.

Now we've been accused of going for the laughs, and for the life of me I can't see the harm in that. All the better, because the greater the laughter, the more chance you have of slipping in the occasional judiciously timed stiletto that says something a little deeper than 'I'm Giving Up Jogging', however pertinent giving up jogging may be to your life. All the same, if your brain is the equivalent of a paint tray, i.e. wide and shallow and all too quickly empty, as mine is, there's no earthly point in trying to bring a message to the world that you simply haven't got. I mean, I admire Proust, but give me P. G. Wodehouse every time.

Besides which, pretty music sweetens the pill. The reason that Gilbert and Sullivan worked so well and their operettas have lasted over the years is that Gilbert's astringent satire was made approachable by Sullivan's exquisite tunes. Laughter is more deadly than vitriol, and graceful music more potent than the sound of hectoring voices.

Occasionally, I suppose I do feel a bit disappointed that I'm not a Brecht or a Buchner, but mostly I'm thankful because I laugh such a lot. So for the time being, I'll plod along with whatever epithets 'they' choose for us, and hopefully the punters will keep laughing.

There is, however, one category that we are consistently put into that drives me crackers, and that's cabaret. Yes, we had our genesis in pub cabaret, but since then we've changed a great deal and we now tour the country playing in theatres with a full two hour show that begins at eight o'clock and lets us finish in time for a drink. Besides, alternative cabaret is much closer to Vaudeville than standard cabaret: people come to see and to listen as they did to see the concert parties of old, whereas cabaret proper is, for both the audience and the performer, utterly different. It's normally on at a much later time than theatre, for a start. People go to eat, have a drink, meet their friends, talk, maybe dance, and seeing a show is in some ways incidental.

Having all been actresses we're happiest in a theatre and besides, our musical roots are in showbiz, not cabaret or popular music. Smoky dives with tables and chairs and people chatting don't suit us at all because our songs have to be listened to to make any sense. They're very wordy, and make terrible background music. Our influences are Coward, Porter, Kern, Lehrer, Sophie Tucker, Mae West, Brecht and Weill, and I would say that we belong firmly and squarely in the world of Vaudeville, if not Burlesque. We're old-fashioned: I don't know why – we just turned out that way. Whenever we appear on television with other performers of our generation, I feel like a refugee from J.R.'s typing pool, so overdressed and over made-up are we, but in the theatre I feel completely at home.

I hate doing television, because it's there that the 'cabaret' categorisation works against us worst of all. Because we sing songs, it would seem that we are ideal to slip into a four minute slot on a chat show or a magazine programme. However, I feel our songs have never worked well in that kind of context, because we have no time to set ourselves or to set the song up properly.

In the live show, the audience has time to get to know us as performers: we gradually reveal our foibles and failings as the evening wears on and we work very hard at the architecture of the

show. If you take one of our songs out of the context of the show
and chuck it ad hoc into a television programme, it doesn't make
sense. 'What on earth are those odd looking women doing?'

However, one has to do television in order to survive. Live theatre
depends on television stars attracting audiences. And in the case of
the documentary, it changed our lives, so I am very grateful to
television in some ways. But if only we could simply perform live
and do occasional documentaries, then how happy I would be.

One of the hardest things to deal with is the price of success. If you
are successful in the entertainment business, you enter the public
domain. You've got to come to terms with the fact that success and
fame go hand-in-hand, no matter how much you dislike or
disapprove of the undignified scrambling after fame's illusory carrots.
In any other profession or trade, you can clamber to the top of your
shrub and bask gently in the warm glow of your colleagues' respect
and/or envy without the rest of the world knowing your business.
But in showbiz, fame equals success and it's quite an alarming
prospect.

Everyone has the right to criticise you, and sometimes the criticism
is extremely painful. I'm not talking now about reviews: they're just
a necessary evil and if we get a bad review, I'm fairly phlegmatic
unless the reviewer is actually inaccurate or fatuous – I got very
irritated at one *Guardian* review which was quite damning because
one of its chief criticisms was that 'Dillie pretends to slug whisky out
of a bottle.' What on earth did the reviewer think actors drink on
stage when doing a drunk scene – *real* whisky? It seemed to be a
facile observation on the part of someone who should have known
better as a regular reviewer of live theatre.

Generally, though, I can take newspaper criticism on the chin.
It's the personal criticism that I find harder to take, and that's
probably a weakness on my part, but I do get angry and hurt when
members of the audience buttonhole us or friends ring up and,
prefacing their comments with 'You know I'm your greatest fan,
but . . .', launch into the most damning and vitriolic tirade against
our latest work/song/show. And the dreadful thing is that they
often mean well. We've been accused of selling out, of being racist,
of being offensive, of being twee, of being too lightweight, of being
too serious, of being too ambitious, of not being whatever it is that
the critic would like us to be.

We can only do what we do. I don't think we're ever going to
break down the frontiers of comedy, but I do think we have
something a bit original, and as long as we do it to the best of our
ability, that's good enough for me. Besides which, there are too

many comedians around who feel that literal honesty is the route to good comedy. Comedy is no good without emotional honesty. Just because someone talks openly about sex or menstruation, it doesn't mean it's going to be funny.

I once talked to an elderly actress who'd years before been in a farce with Athene Seyler, the grand old lady of comedy. This actress had a small but very funny part, and one of her best laugh lines was when she had to ask for a cup of tea.

For the first few weeks, she got the laugh every single time she asked for that cup of tea. Then, without any apparent reason, the laugh stopped coming. She got desperate, and tried the line all sorts of different ways, but with no success. The laugh had gone.

At length, she went to Athene Seyler for help. 'Miss Seyler,' she said, 'I'm not getting that laugh on the cup of tea line any more. What am I doing wrong?'

Very gently, Athene Seyler said to the actress, 'It's because you're asking for a laugh, my dear, instead of a cup of tea.' She got the laugh back that night.

So, with that story firmly in mind, we always try as much as possible to be first of all honest to the audience, and secondly true to ourselves.

The current team seems to be well settled. I think that Adèle, Nica and I will probably go on working together for some years now. And last year we changed agents again and moved, with the incomparable Rachel, to the Noel Gay Management who are ideally suited to looking after us, and are now more like a family than anything.

We definitely couldn't continue without Nica: no other director would put their heart and soul into the group the way she does all year round. She's so many things besides being the director: mother, mentor, friend, agony aunt, psychiatrist, boss – I don't know how she puts up with us. We're very lucky indeed.

Finally, I think we've had the luckiest attribute of all: the luck to be able to recognise luck when we see it.

And one of our nicest moments came when Rachel showed us a sheaf of letters that came from the managers of some of the theatres we played at last year.

One by one, they all thanked us for a hugely successful show and packing their theatres, and almost all of them said that they'd never ever seen such a mixture of age, class and type in the theatre at one time.

That makes it all worthwhile.

SONG OF THE HOMESICK TRAVELLER

When you're far away from ye'er ane countree
　From all your kith and kin that you hold dear:
When there's ne'er a soul that ye can call ye'er friend
　And all the world seems sae dark and drear.
When ye'er hairt is sair and weary
　And ye long once mair tae see ye'er home:
That's when I hear a voice keep calling me,
　Calling me nae mair tae roam:

Little Chef, I hear you calling
'Cross the waves, ye call tae me:
For 'tis those mixed grills and not the highland hills
That mean home sweet home tae me.

Well at Heston and at the Watford Gap
　'Tis nae wonder all the fold wear frowns:
For the food they sairve ye there is awfu' pap,
　Unlike the Little Chef's sublime hash browns.
There's a shop that sell ye lovely souvenirs —
　They always do their best tae please:
And their hygiene standards are unbeatable,
　Ev'ry hour they check the lavat'ries . . .

Little Chef, I hear you calling,
Your free map is in ma car:
Cheery waitresses
In their gingham dresses
And ye'er table mats show where ye are.

Little Chef, I hear you calling,
You are owned by T.H.F.
Life is so much sweeter
Than at Happy Eater . . .
How I love you Little Chef.

Words: Adèle Anderson, Dillie Keane
Music: Dillie Keane
© 1985

LAST 4 BARS OF LAST CHORUS (to be sung with great passion.)

LIFE is SO MUCH SWEETER THAN AT HAPPY EAT-ER, HOW I LOVE YE, LIT-TLE CHEF

On the road, the digs are sometimes very comfortable.

A night on the tiles: After lunching at the Little Chef, Adèle dines out with His Highness Donitri Macphersonov, a diminutive exiled prince, at trendy Smith's Restaurant of fashionable Covent Garden. Agent Rachel Swann (whose escort is in the toilet) is ordering champagne and oysters as always. Dillie's date has not yet materialised.

Crossword Answers

Across
1. Lieder
5. Feathers
9. Kilo
10. Seed
12. Ills
14. Glues
16. Wry
17. Deign
19. Hurl
22. Ogle
23. Ore
24. Octaves
25. Nay
28. Fascinating Aïda
31. Pit
33. Arrange
34. Awl
36. Obit

38. Aria
39. Lines
41. Emu
42. Prang
43. Sate
44. Tomb
45. 31 down Nail polish
46. Hilarity
47. Moscow

Down
1. Laugh off
2. Ensure
3. Ekes
4. Rid
5. Four part harmony
6. Told
7. Ensign
8. Sidney

11. Eel
13. Leo
15. Lur
18. Gland
20. Scenery
21. Teenage
26. Act
27. Van
29. Alibi
30. All aglow
31. see 45 across
32. Tinsel
34. Arabic
35. Win
37. Tea
38. Arm
40. Star
42. Polo
44. Tim

THE DIRECTOR ALWAYS HAS THE LAST WORD

People often ask me, with a look of sympathy and understanding: 'What's it like working with three women (sigh)?'

It would be more appropriate to ask what's it like working with three completely different, intelligent, talented, strong-minded performers.

Heaven and Hell at once.

Fascinating Aïda are a pretty emotional cocktail: we argue, get tense, cry in extremis and all want our own way. But our relationship is based on a bedrock of support and encouragement for each other: we want everyone to be good. So if someone's being unreasonable in rehearsal because the man in their life's just walked out, we empathise and cope with it. After all, we've all been there. The female reviewer who criticised the act for the bitchiness on stage that 'proved the age old theory that women can't work together' is talking through her hat. That's the cliché of women working together, and it's a shame that a gag on stage is assumed to be the nature of the beast. All the great male double acts from Laurel and Hardy to Morecambe and Wise have been based on the tension of one-upmanship, yet with women it's called bitchiness.

As Director, I have a special place. For a start, I don't have to live with Dillie, Adèle and Marilyn: they spend more time with each other than with their lovers. Very hard. Secondly, I'm Out Front. However clever the performer is they can't be aware of how the incredibly funny bit of business they're doing (or so they think) is actually coming over to the audience.

Fascinating Aïda is a very creative team. That's why we argue so much. But at the end of the day it's up to me to make the final decisions and this I do despite the efforts of friends, well-wishers and Mrs Keane to interfere. ('Does Dillie's dress have to be so revealing?') My job is to ensure that, whilst allowing each individual talent to be shown off at its best, the show is well balanced between the three. I have to take an overall view and get their stage relationship right. The great thing about Fascinating Aïda is that there is room for each individual talent, and there's nothing I like more than mingling with the audience in the interval and hearing them argue as to which one's the best.

So how do we prepare a show? It doesn't come magically out of the air as some members of the audience think. ('Do you practise?')

We rehearse a *lot*.

First of all we discuss the numbers we'd like to include. A tricky one, this. I'm lucky as Dillie is very prolific and I have the choice of a lot of material. That's unusual in this line of business. Some performers do the same show for years. It's also very hard to decide how many old favourites we should keep in. Take 'The Herpes Tango' for instance. Audiences love it and miss it if we don't do it. We feel a need to change our shows but don't want to disappoint our audiences or replace an 'A' song with one that's perhaps not quite as good. So we try to strike a balance with a mixture of old and new.

The songs we're thinking of doing are learnt. We discuss the approach we're going to take, and then I set the dance movements. Sometimes it takes a lot of work to get a number right. We got into

Nica as rehearsals progress.

very deep water with 'Taboo' and tried it about six different ways before it worked. Now it's a hoary old chestnut. Similarly, 'England O England' started out as a calypso and ended up as an unaccompanied folk song with Morris Dance. That was a prime example of good creative collaboration. I liked the lyrics (which the three of them had co-written) but Dillie wasn't sure of the music. I came up with a different approach, and she then re-wrote the tune.

We have to polish and polish the numbers under consideration. I usually take them off to the Pineapple Dance Centre for a few sessions in front of the mirrors. It's amazing how fast their movement improves when they can see exactly what they look like. Sometimes we have to try the numbers in costume as I expect them to do all sorts of wonderful things in their high heels and chi-chi frocks. Could *you* tap dance in your favourite ball gown?

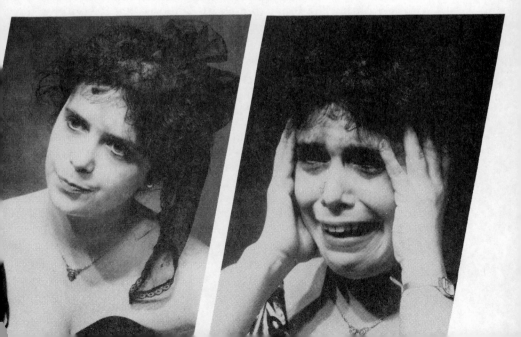

Nica improvises with a prop. (Note that Nica also dresses up for rehearsal.)

The order is the next vital thing. A song in the wrong place ca weaken both the song and the order enormously and ruin t balance of the show. In the right place – bingo! By this stage we' beginning to get the feel of the whole show and can start writing t links. These form a bridge between the songs and 'get us in' to t next song or sequence of songs. Sometimes these take the form chat, sometimes we set up a short sketch and/or perform a visu gag. Dillie does most of these links: it's one of the few chances s gets to get away from the piano. She's also the best at it, as Maril and Adèle would agree.

As the group has developed and got better at what it do whatever that may be, we've extended the visual jokes. Dillie, particular, has been rediscovering her clown and I love worki with her on it. The great thing with Dillie is that if you give her comic idea, she'll do wonderful things with it which a lot performers simply couldn't do. A perfect example is her Plant Ga which, I'm sure, will be in the show for a long time.

We were opening a new show at the Lyric Hammersmit Everything had gone wrong with the lights – the lighting design was also lighting a show at the Liverpool Playhouse at the same tin and had spent most of the afternoon on the phone while we grop around in the semi-darkness, and we obviously weren't going to g our promised dress rehearsal. At 7.00 pm I was in the bar having it'll-be-all-right-on-the-night, it's-not-worth-committing-suicide drir when Marilyn rushed up saying she needed a three minute cover get out of her crinoline in the wings after her solo before she'd ready for the next number. We already had a gag at the end of h big solo where Dillie was presented with a bouquet of flowe supposedly intended for Marilyn. I was standing there panicki when my eyes alighted on the big plastic plants dotted all round the foyer and bar. Pushing several innocent members of the public aside, I shouted at the manager 'We're borrowing this!' and grabbed the biggest plant. The idea was to extend the joke with the bouquet into a longer gag with Dillie then being presented with this enormous tree as well as the bunch of flowers and being stuck on stage with it. It was literally thrown at her minutes before she was due to go on. We played with it, she experimented with several ideas and we finally ended up with a long sequence where she got her head stuck between the branches and then proceeded to play the piano with her arms around the trunk. It was very funny, Marilyn got her three minutes cover and we found a wonderful visual gag which we now get into each show.

I can't always guarantee such inspiration, nor the decor of whatever theatre we might happen to find ourselves in!

So finally, we end up with a script. Somewhere along the line we've decided on costumes, which is another story – the Fascinating Aïda Frock Finding Expeditions would need a whole chapter. We usually discuss this early on in the proceedings. Then I tell the lighting designer what I want in terms of lights – I don't always get it – as we often use lighting jokes, e.g. a mirror ball in 'Sew on a Sequin' to add an extra visual comic element. Normally at this stage Dillie and I have our only major row. She's convinced I get too carried away and that the audience can't see her, and she demands more light. The stage crew get embarrassed and go for a pint. Several furious exchanges later some sort of compromise is reached, Dillie making a mental note to nobble the lighting operator and get the lights taken up several points, me making a mental note to see him after her and get them back down again!

Then we're ready to face the trickiest and most unknown element of all – the audience. Now it's up to FA. My worst moment. Now is not the time to relax – what wonderfully obvious ad lib might Dillie miss? What might Adèle do with her feet? Will Marilyn be able to move in her new dress? Will Dillie stay in her new dress? Will the lighting operator get the cues right? Will . . . oh, the possible pitfalls are many especially as, despite my wonderful planning, we haven't had quite enough time . . . And most important of all – will *they* laugh?

So I sit somewhere in the depths of the audience, shaking, my stomach in my shoes, shoulders hunched, a bundle of nerves. The only things saving my sanity are my two secret weapons – my note book and my pen. I sometimes wish they were wearing studio headphones so they could have a little voice in their ear: Marilyn, wrong foot! Adèle, don't move *yet*! Dillie, slow down . . . Instead, my pen flies across the paper noting down the errors, usually completely unnoticed by the audience (thank you, God) but standing out like neon signs to me. Then as the laughs come in, relief floods through me and I think 'It's going to be all right. They're enjoying it. I'm not going to have to kill myself.'

After the show, we'll have a quick session with my notes and then sleep on it. Audience reaction may mean we try some of the patter a slightly different way but, like anything else, we've got better and better at judging what will and won't work. But a show is like a car: it needs to run in and it takes time to get the timing exactly right and play the audience properly. The show will change slightly with every audience and also develop over a period of time as it's performed. That's a good thing in this type of work. It's not like playing a long run of a play or a musical: the girls are playing themselves for a large part of the show as opposed to 'a character' and they must have some freedom within that to interpret and develop things in their own way. I would be doing my job badly if I drilled them to the stage where I was denying them their artistic freedom: I believe that you can still be polished while retaining a large degree of spontaneity. It just wouldn't be as good if they didn't have any room to play around with the show within a tight structure.

I'll watch each new show every night for the first week. Things may be amended slightly and we'll have a notes session daily. Then I hand it over to them whilst they go off to all points of the compass and I get on with running my theatre. But we always keep in close touch and I help make a lot of the planning decisions. Fascinating Aïda is a year round job for me and a deep personal commitment.

I love working with them: it's a fulfilling two-way creative flow. I get first class material to work with, and we have a very happy, if occasionally fraught, relationship.

Long may it last.

GOODBYE AND GO

or Bugger off, we want to get to the bar before it closes, too

Fascinating Who?

© Adèle Anderson and
Dillie Keane 1985

Your night is drawing to a close
But ours has just begun
You're off to seek some sweet repose
We're out to have some fun
Our dressing room is thronged with beaux
Whose manly hearts we've won
They'll take us where the champagne flows
Until the morning sun

SO

Why don't you go?
Then we can go
Out where we go every night

We've done our stuff
It must be enough
Please *don't* make us suffer, all right?

You have been so inspiring
But singing all night is so damned tiring
And, what is more, we are all perspiring

So into the showers
Or in a few hours
Just like our flowers we will *die*

Boy, are we spent
It's time we went
So ladies and gents — GOODBYE

Words: Adèle Anderson
Music: Dillie Keane and Adèle Anderson
© 1985